John Sturges

Considerations on the Present State of the Church-Establishment

In Letters to the Right Reverend the Lord Bishop of London

John Sturges

Considerations on the Present State of the Church-Establishment
In Letters to the Right Reverend the Lord Bishop of London

ISBN/EAN: 9783337002718

Printed in Europe, USA, Canada, Australia, Japan

Cover: Foto ©Lupo / pixelio.de

More available books at **www.hansebooks.com**

CONSIDERATIONS

ON THE

PRESENT STATE

OF THE

CHURCH-ESTABLISHMENT,

IN LETTERS

TO

THE RIGHT REVEREND THE

LORD BISHOP OF LONDON.

By JOHN STURGES, M.A.
PREBENDARY OF WINCHESTER,
AND CHAPLAIN IN ORDINARY TO HIS MAJESTY.

LONDON
Printed for T. CADELL, in the Strand.

C O N T E N T S.

A 2 LETTER

L E T T E R VI.

L E T T E R VII.

L E T T E R VIII.

LETTER I.

INTRODUCTION.

My Lord,

THE long suspension of religious controversies between the different denominations of Protestants in this country, the uninterrupted liberty and security with which all of them have professed their respective opinions, and exercised their respective modes of worship, and the terms of amity which have for the most part appeared to subsist between them and the Established Church, had I believe produced a general persuasion; that as we were all grown wiser

B   about

about the fubjects on which we differed formerly, fo we were grown more reafonable, liberal, and benevolent with refpect to thofe things, on which we may ftill differ; that there was little reafon to apprehend a revival of diffentions and animofities, which are always the effect of prejudice and paffion, and on religious fubjects are peculiarly unbecoming.

I confefs, I am difappointed in feeing even a fingle inftance of that fpirit, which I had flattered myfelf had been totally extinguifhed. That people fhould be of one mind in matters of religion, either with refpect to the fubftantial part of it, or the form in which it is to be adminiftered, a very moderate knowledge of human nature will teach us never to expect; but that notwithftanding thefe differences men fhould treat each other without bitternefs, with moderation and candor,

candor, is an expectation, which in thefe times I fhould have thought not quite unreafonable. I proteft, my Lord, when I now hear of * ' our venerating ' furplices, gowns, caffocks, and hoods; ' † when I fee every kind of civil and reli- ' gious evil charged to the account of ' Epifcopacy; and am told ‡, that all Hu- ' man Legiflation is oppreffive to con- ' fcience;' I feel myfelf ready to believe, that we are fet backward in the world three or four generations; and can with difficulty be perfuaded, that we are in truth advancing towards the end of the eighteenth century.

---

* Plan of Lectures on the Principles of Non-con- formity, for the inftruction of Catechumens. By R. Robinfon. Approved by the Eaftern Affociation at Harlow, Effex, and figned, by order of all, by the Moderator. Lect. 5.

† Lect. 3. throughout.

‡ Lect. 9.

Intem-

Intemperate Cenſure is not fitted either to convince or to conciliate reaſonable inquirers; but it has led me, as it probably may others, to reflect on the ſubject with ſome attention, and to conſider, diveſting myſelf as much as I could of a natural partiality to a Church of which I am a Member, and a Profeſſion to which I belong, how far our Eccleſiaſtical Eſtabliſhment, as it now ſubſiſts in this country, is an Inſtitution fit for the purpoſes it was meant to anſwer, both with reſpect to Religion and Society; how far the Clergy of England are worthy Miniſters of the Religion of Chriſt, and uſeful Members of our Civil Community.

The Principles, on which Eſtabliſhments in general, and our own in particular are founded; the Tolerating Spirit of the Church of England with reſpect to Chriſtians of other denominations; the Juriſdiction

Jurifdiction affigned to it by the Laws of our Country; the Provifion made for its Clergy; their Learning and Freedom of Inquiry; our Public Forms in which they officiate, their Duties, and their Manners, are particulars, which naturally offer themfelves on this fubject. But it is a fubject, my Lord, like all others, where human inftitutions and numerous bodies of men are concerned, in which it is fruitlefs, it would argue only an ignorance of our nature, to expect abfolute perfection. Comparative merit is all, that the beft governments and wifeft inftitutions can claim; imperfections and defects will in all the works of man every where occur to us; time and a change of circumftances will produce them, where they did not originally exift; and we muft be fatisfied with thofe inftitutions, where they are the feweft and leaft; we muft be contented to efteem thofe excellent,

B 3   where

where they are mixed with what is good and valuable only in a fmall proportion.

Permit me, my Lord, to addrefs the reflections I have been led to form on this fubject to your Lordfhip; the eminence of your ftation in the Church, and the eminence of your character in that ftation, will I hope give this addrefs fome propriety.

LETTER

LETTER II.

On Establishments in general, and that of the Church of England in particular.

WITH some persons, my Lord, the word *Establishment* is itself criminal; they reprobate all Human Authority, all Human Opinions, which respect religion, as unlawful; as infringing their own liberty, and derogating from the Supremacy of Christ. I will beg leave to state the principles, on which, according to my conceptions, all Religious Societies must be founded; and shall endeavour to shew, that all, which are designed for any permanency, (for a congregation in a field, which never meets again, is not worth calling a society) must in effect admit, whatever they may

B 4 profess

profefs to do, Human Authority for their regulation, muft concur in Human Opinions as a bond of union; and that Eftablifhments, as fuch, are not on that account unlawful; inconfiftent with our liberty as men, with our allegiance to Chrift as Chriftians.

Such authority may be ill-employed, fuch opinions may be ill-founded, and improperly impofed; violence may be exerted by the one, in order to enforce the other; by their abufe they may both become pernicious; but it no more follows from thence, that the principle on which they are ufed is unlawful, than that, becaufe there are in the world many bad Civil Laws, therefore all Legiflation is unjuft.

If Religion were to fubfift only in the hearts of individuals without the con-
currence

currence of others, or any external profeſſion of it; if God had not meant, that
in this inſtance, as well as in all others, we
ſhould be Social Creatures, the Truths and
Precepts, which we collect by our reaſon,
and which are delivered to us by revelation,
would then in their naked ſtate be ſufficient to make us in this manner religious:
we might certainly think of God as we
pleaſed, and offer to him in what manner we pleaſed our ſolitary worſhip. But
if we are not ſatisfied with that, if we
are prompted by our nature to unite with
others in the adoration of the Supreme
Being, and feel our religion imperfect
without doing ſo, we muſt in ſome re-
ſpects agree with thoſe others; there
muſt be ſome mutual compliances; and
certain regulations muſt be admitted,
both with reſpect to the Outward Form of
Worſhip, and the Opinions conveyed by
it,

Without

Without some regulations of the Outward Form in which the Worshippers are agreed, it is impossible that Public Worship can subsist even in its simplest shape; and as the reason of this worship, the manner of our addressing God, and the duties which we suppose him to require from us, arise from the Opinions we form concerning him, concerning his attributes and government, it is plain, that without a certain Agreement in these opinions it is impossible for different persons to join in the worship of God, and in giving or receiving Religious Instruction, which usually makes part of it. A Jew or a Christian could not join with an old Heathen in worshipping his numerous and imaginary deities. A Protestant cannot concur with a Papist in offering his prayers to the Virgin Mary, to Angels, and to Saints. The same prayers also, and the same instruction, cannot well

suit

suit thofe Proteftants, who differ about the Object of their worfhip, or about the Neceffity of good works to falvation.

Every United Set of Worfhippers muft therefore agree in certain Forms and Opinions; and they muft make fuch Agreement the condition, on which others may be admitted to their Society. They muft prefcribe, like all other focieties, thefe conditions for themfelves; and thofe, who do not chufe to comply with them, muft either not enter into fuch a fociety, or retire from it.

'But this, it is faid, is an infringe-
'ment of our Liberty, an oppreffion
'of Confcience; it is ufurping the Su-
'premacy of Chrift; and giving Human
'Opinions that authority, which is only
'due to Divine Revelation.'

That

That Abfolute Liberty is inconfiftent with every fpecies of fociety, whether civil or religious, is moft certain; it can only belong to detached, infulated individuals. The moment we begin to act in concert with any of our fellow-creatures, this liberty is narrowed; we muft fubmit to fome rules, and be content to lie under certain reftraints with refpect to others, which it is neceffary for our own good that they fhould lie under with refpect to ourfelves. The Liberty of the Freeft States never was and never can be more than this; it can only be a Qualified Liberty, as great as is confiftent, not with the good of any one citizen, but of all taken together. And when in any fort of fociety this is poffeffed in fuch a degree, every wife man knows, that he poffeffes all which can from the nature of things be had. If there be any, who chufe to prefer to it the Abfolute Liberty

5   of

of a folitary State of nature, with them I
will not reafon; but leave them to find
in that ftate an equivalent for all the
bleffings of Society.

'But Confcience is oppreffed by fuch
'conditions.' What, if it be in the
power of him, who diflikes them, not
to oblige himfelf to the obfervance of
them? if he be at liberty not to make
part of that fociety, which requires it?
Can any injury be done; can the confcience of any be wounded, where the
contract is voluntary; where this alter-
native is offered, either enter into fuch a
fociety and accept the conditions of it;
or abftain from the one, and be exempt
from the other?

'The interpofition alfo of Human Au-
'thority in matters of Religion is ufurp-
'ing the Supremacy of Chrift.' But
without

without certain Regulations no Societies can exist; as the Societies are Human, the regulations made for them must be by Human Authority. We find in the Scriptures the doctrines and precepts of our religion; they are there offered to the reader, who may make what use of them he pleases; who will understand them in that sense, which shall approve itself to his mind. But if many persons chuse to join in an external Profession of this religion, this profession must be administered in a certain form, and by certain persons; the naked Doctrines and Precepts will not administer themselves any more, than the abstract Idea of Justice will be sufficient to answer the purposes of a State, without applying it, making it effectual, and giving as it were a body to it, by laws.

Whatever Regulations are made for Christian Churches, are supposed and
professed

profeſſed by thoſe who make them, to
be agreeable to the commands of Chriſt,
to be the means of carrying thoſe commands into execution. Is this uſurp-
ing Chriſt's authority? We all, I preſume, acknowledge God to be the Supreme Governor of the world. We are
all I ſuppoſe ready to allow, that it is
from him we derive our notions of Juſtice; that it is his will we ſhould exerciſe this virtue towards our fellow-creatures. But did any reaſonable man ever
conclude from hence, that making Laws
for the purpoſes of Practical Juſtice
amongſt men was impious with reſpect
to God, was intrenching on his ſove-
reignty? The truth is, that without
the interpoſition of Human Authority, in
its different degrees, Public Religion and
Public Juſtice could not ſubſiſt.

There

' There remains another charge on Esta-blifhments, ' that they impofe on men ' Human Opinions, and give them an ' Authority, which is only due to Divine ' Revelation.' It has been faid before, and is indifputable, that a certain Agree-ment of Opinions with refpect to God is neceffary for thofe, who would join in religious worfhip. Now, who is to be judge for any given Society, what thofe opinions fhall be ? The Society muft undoubtedly judge for itfelf. The warmeft advocates for Religious Liberty plead for the right of Private Judgement; that men fhould be permitted to judge for themfelves. Nothing is more in-conteftible. And fhall not a Society have the fame right of judging for it-felf ? Is this commendable in an indi-vidual, and unlawful in a Society ? They may both be miftaken in forming their opinions; this is the confequence of hu-

man

man infirmity; but they are both the only and the proper judges for themselves.

And this Judgement on Religious Subjects must be exercised; for men will differ about them, and the Scriptures, which we all allow to be the Revelation of God, will no more interpret themselves, than the doctrines contained, teach; or the duties prescribed in them, execute themselves. Each Society therefore will adopt those Opinions, which seem to them true; and they will be, like all other conclusions of our minds on the subjects proposed to them, Human Opinions; they must and can be no other.

These, my Lord, are the principles on which, according to my conceptions, all Religious Societies must be founded; that

C   they

they are lawful, I think is undoubted; and pretty apparent, that they are necessary. For we shall find those Sects of Christians, who most disclaim Human Authority and Human Opinions, if we attend to things themselves rather than to the names by which they are called, are, in fact, from the necessity of the case, whatever they may profess, obliged to use them both. The minute regulations of a single Independent Congregation, to which the Members of it must conform about the time, place, and manner of worship, are the same in *kind* with the numerous Laws of an Established National Church, and differ only in *degree*; it is all of it Human Authority. The Opinions by which the different Congregations of Dissenters are distinguished from one another, and from the Established Church, are in effect the Confessions of Faith of

those

thofe Congregations *; and thefe all confift of Human Opinions. The truth is,
neither We or They are in fault for ufing
thefe Human Inftruments; it is a matter
not of choice, but of neceffity; fuch is
the nature God has given us, that without them Men cannot be made to act together; there can be no Society, either
Civil or Religious.

I have been led, my Lord, thus far in
difcuffing thefe Firft Principles, becaufe
they affect our own Eftablifhment in
common with all others; though it was
not fo much the intention of thefe Letters, which I take the liberty of addreffing to your Lordfhip, to controvert the

* In fome Congregations the Minifter makes his
own Confeffion in form; in all it muft be underftood; for there muft be a certain Agreement between him and his Congregation.
     See Prot. Diff. Catechifm, Part ii. Quef. 93.

Forms and Opinions of other Churches,
as to confider the Prefent State and Circumftances of our Own. Before we
looked at the Superftruĉture, it feemed
but reafonable to examine whether the
Foundation was as unfound and infecure,
as fome writers by their confident affer-
tions would endeavour to perfuade us.
But the Foundation, my Lord, is good;
the Rights, which the Church of England exercifes with refpeĉt to her own
Forms and Opinions, are Rights which
muft belong to Every Church; fhe does
not violate thofe of other Churches, or
of Individuals, by forcing men into her
pale againft their confent; fhe claims no
independence, no exemption from the
power of the Civil Magiftrate; and
makes no pretenfions to Infallibility.

Without Toleration no Eftablifhment
can be lawful, can be defenfible. The
Right

Right of any Church to chufe her own
Forms and to fettle her own Opinions
can only be maintained (and in what I
have already faid has only been maintained) on the footing of leaving others
to enjoy the fame Right without injury
or moleftation; of letting them worfhip
and teach as they pleafe, provided their
worfhip and teaching be not hurtful to
the State; in which cafe only the Civil
Magiftrate can juftly interpofe. But the
Tolerating Spirit of our Church is a matter of fuch importance in the prefent inquiry, and Toleration has been enjoyed
in this country fo completely in the prefent age, that it well deferves to be the
fubject of a feparate letter, to which I
beg leave to referve it.

Civil Government is imperfect, is un-
able to effect the purpofes for which it is
defigned, if all fects, all focieties of

men

men be not equally subject to its authority. Of this authority the Church of England does not wish to be independent; she sets up no spiritual claims of disobedience. Our earlier History abounds with the mischiefs arising from the incompatible powers of a Pope and a Civil Government; the dissentions, the wars, the miseries, which arose from hence, are familiar to us; and we are from habit apt to consider the principle of Ecclesiastical Independence as peculiar to Popery. It was indeed maintained by that Church more openly, and more desperately, (for there was no species of political wickedness that was not employed to maintain it) than by any other; but it is not confined to that alone; it may subsist under other forms, and be the ruling maxim of other Churches, which profess to be the furthest removed from Popery: but wherever it be found

it

it is hoftile to Civil Government, and deferves to be treated as fuch by the Magiftrate who is the fupporter of it.

The Church of England regulates her own Forms and declares her own Opinions; but in fo doing fhe lays no claim to Infallibility. She judges for herfelf, as an Individual does, and acts accordingly. She fuppofes herfelf right, as every Individual muft do, when he acts to the beft of his judgement; but does not treat others, as if they were neceffarily in the wrong *. Whatever is faid in our Articles of her Authority can amount to no more than this; it can be interpreted no otherwife confiftently with other paffages of the fame Articles, and

* See Art. 6, 20, and 34; and Hoadly's Anfwer to the Reprefentation of the Committee of the Lower Houfe, &c.

Works, Vol. ii. p. 483.

the

the general principles of the Reformation, on which they were framed,
' Every Church, as has been already
' said, muſt have Power to decree Rites
' and Ceremonies' for herſelf and for
her own uſe, ' and Authority in Contro-
' verſies of Faith ;' that is, a power of
declaring her judgement, in order to determine, what her ſenſe of Scripture is,
and her interpretation of it, concerning them. This is a power conſiſtent,
as the Church of England profeſſes it to
be, with the ſupreme authority of Scripture ; and which is in fact exerted, from
the neceſſity of the caſe, by thoſe Congregations, who moſt diſclaim it.

The Principles then, my Lord, on
which our Eſtabliſhment is founded, I apprehend to be unexceptionable ; whether
in the application of theſe we have been

fo fortunate in all refpects, is a matter
that will admit of more difpute.

As to mere Forms and Ceremonies, I
fhould have thought all controverfy about
them had been at an end, if I had not
been lately convinced of the contrary.
Opinions are a fubject of more confequence; and as it is undoubted, that the
Members, and efpecially the Minifters of
a Church, muft to a certain degree concur in them; fo it is no lefs true, that
fuch being the neceffity, a Public Collection of thefe Opinions, for the purpofe of Uniformity, fhould be as fhort,
as plain, and as comprehenfive, as the
end propofed will admit; that the Members of a Church may not be loaded with
unneceffary conditions, or others be un-
neceffarily excluded from it.

In

In a large collection of Speculative Opinions, obfcure and difputable by their nature, it is impoflible, that great numbers of perfons can perfectly agree; agree I mean after full inquiry and examination; fome will acquiefce without making fuch inquiry, others will diffemble, and all perhaps will think themfelves entitled to ufe a latitude, that is not fo much authorifed by the terms in which their Affent is expreffed, as by the general principles of our nature and the conftitution of our mind. In the mean time the end propofed will not be anfwered; and it is probably unneceffary, that it fhould: Unanimity in that degree will never in fact be produced.

As Chriftianity alfo fhould be made as much as poffible in the public profeffion of it, what it is in itfelf, a Religion of

bene-

benevolence and concord, Chriftians fhould be invited by every conciliating, every accommodating meafure to join in one profeffion; all invidious diftinctions, all unneceffary impediments fhould be re-moved; fmaller differences fhould be dropped by all parties, provided that in greater things they can be made to agree. Now to multiply the Public Opinions, by which one Church is diftinguifhed from others, on thofe fubjects efpecially which are difficult and difputable, is to multiply the conditions required from thofe who would accede to it, and to make their union with it lefs practicable.

I confefs, my Lord, that our Articles appear liable to thefe objections; the par-ticulars of them are too numerous; the fubjects of fome of them of a moft ob-fcure and difputable kind, where it may feem unneceffary and perhaps improper to

go

go fo far in defining; on both thefe accounts the Affent required from our Clergy may appear too ftrict, and other Chriftians may be difcouraged from joining in communion with us.

That fuch Objections fhould now lie to our Articles, is what might reafonably have been expected, notwithftanding all the abilities of the perfons who compiled them, notwithftanding all their merits in the common caufe of Proteftant Chriftianity. Men were at that time in fome meafure new to the fubject of Church-Eftablifhments; they had not formed juft notions of Religious Liberty; and Toleration was neither underftood or practifed. Thefe topics have been fince difcuffed with freedom and ability; religious prejudices have worn off, and the prefent modes of thinking are become more liberal and tolerant. They did as much

as

as could be expected from them; and if
their System be compared with thofe of
other Reformers in the fame age, the
comparifon would probably turn out
much to their advantage; but this is no
reafon, why their work fhould not be
corrected and improved at a fubfequent
period, when we are poffeffed of great
advantages, and furnifhed with confiderable means of improvement.

Such a Revifion, my Lord, both of
our Articles and Forms, undertaken at a
proper time, when the public fituation
of our country will admit of attention
to thefe internal concerns of it, under
the authority of the State, by the Governors of our Church, the Succeffors of
thefe venerable Reformers, and conducted
as it would then be with fobriety and
good fenfe, would much contribute to
her interefts and honour; the eafe of her

own

own Minifters would be confulted by it,
many objections removed, and the good
opinion of reafonable and moderate men
of all parties conciliated.

Might I prefume, my Lord, to ftate,
what appears to me the proper ground for
forming a Confeffion of Faith, for draw-
ing the line of Separation between one
Chriftian Society and another? Every
Church will, as fhe has a right, judge
for herfelf with refpect to her own Opinions. But whatever thofe Opinions are,
the leading and moft important only,
what fhe judges *effential* to True Chriftianity, fhould be felected and brought
forth for Public Ufe; where to diftinguifh
and fubdivide is unfit and pernicious.
Speculative men in private may do this as
they pleafe; in public it only marks out
and multiplies differences. The Bafis of
every Eftablifhment fhould be made as
broad

broad as poffible, that all, who agree in
great points, may be comprehended in it.
Thefe ftriking features, thefe leading
principles. of our Religion are all that
fhould be expreffed in Forms of Public
Worfhip; they comprife all the Neceffary
Subjects of Public Inftruction.

Now as the reafon of requiring from
Minifters an approbation of the Opinions
of their Church, is to obtain affurance
from them, of their being qualified to
officiate in the prefcribed Forms of Public
Worfhip, and of their conforming to
thofe Opinions in their Public Inftruction;
whatever makes no part either of the one
or the other, fhould alfo make no part
of a Confeffion of Faith; it has nothing
to do with the object of it. The Forms
indeed of Public Worfhip will neceffarily
contain in them, either expreffed or im-
plied, all the Doctrines, which are meant

to

to be the fubjects of Public Inftruction. The Confeffion of Faith therefore and the Liturgy of a Church fhould be Counter-parts to each other; their relation is mutual; if the former contain lefs than the latter, it is deficient; if more, it is redundant; and it is from this redundancy, that reafonable objections are moft likely to arife.

If therefore that Form of Public Worfhip be the beft, which, confiftently with the Opinions of the Church who prefcribes it, is the moft fimple, the moft intelligible, the moft comprehenfive; that Confeffion of Faith, which moft exactly correfponds to this Form, will be the beft likewife.

LETTER

LETTER III.

On *the Tolerating Spirit of the Church of England.*

I HAVE already faid, my Lord, ' that without Toleration no Eftablifhment can be lawful or defenfible ; that the Right of any Church to chufe her own Forms and to fettle her own Opinions can only be maintained on the footing of leaving others to enjoy the fame right without injury or moleftation ; of letting them worfhip and teach as they pleafe, provided their worfhip and teaching be not hurtful to the State, in which cafe only the Civil Magiftrate can juftly interpofe.' To make others think and believe what You chufe to prefcribe, is impoffible ; to make them profefs fuch

D   Opinions

Opinions and Belief, which they have not; to make them obferve religious Forms founded on thefe, which they efteem unlawful or difapprove, is unjuft. But when thofe, who diffent from the majority in thefe things, have the liberty, not of thinking and believing as they pleafe, for this cannot be taken from them, but of, expreffing thefe opinions and belief by Public Religious Worfhip, as they fhall chufe; (the fecurity of the State being always prefuppofed) they have every thing, which reafon and juftice can require.

Yet it is furprifing, how long men have been in acknowledging principles fo reafonable and obvious. When the Proteftant world broke loofe from Popery, they felt indeed fufficiently from recent and cruel experience the fevere tyranny, to which they had been fo long fubject. It was natural to fuppofe, that they would

immediately

Immediately renounce thofe principles,
which had been the foundation of it.
They abjured the Supremacy of the Pope,
and rejected the abfurd religious tenets of
his Church; but to grant men liberty in
matters of Religion, feemed not once to
occur to them; the different Sects had
no notion of Chriftianity in any other
form than their own, and in this they
thought it lawful to oblige all others to
concur. Popery, as their common enemy
and of the moft dangerous kind, was
treated, and juftly treated, by all with
moft feverity; but there is no reafon to
commend the conduct of the Proteftant
parties towards each other; almoft every
one of them was in its turn intolerant;
and as they were poffeffed of power, inflicted
on thofe, who differed from them, injuries,
not perhaps quite the fame in degree with
thofe inflicted by the Church of Rome,
but the fame in kind, and to be juftified

only

only on the fame principles. A ftriking inftance this of the flow and difficult ad-miffion of Truth into the Human Mind, when the accefs is fhut againft it by the love of power, by falfe notions of intereft, and by old prejudices. *

Thefe

* Another inftance of this, and of men's incon-fiftency with their own principles, was the conftant oppofition of America, to the admiffion of Bifhops for the fpiritual purpofes of the Church of England in that country; for I have ever underftood, and moft affuredly believe, they were intended for thefe only. This I think appears from Archbifhop Secker's words quoted in Dr. Furneaux's Letters to Blackftone, p. 191, 2d. edit. with the defign of fhewing the con-trary. " The propofal is (faith the Archbifhop) " that the Bifhops fhall exercife fuch jurifdiction " *over the Clergy of the Church of England in thofe parts,* " as the late Bifhop of London's Commiffaries did, " *or fuch as it might be thought proper that any future* " *Commiffaries fhould,* if this defign were not to take " place." The latter words are marked with Italics by Dr. Furneaux; the former by me; for if the

Jurif-

' These intolerant principles, common to almost all denominations of Christians, were encouraged by the unhappy civil diffentions, with which in this country they were connected. Popery may be considered, from the Reformation to the times within our own memory, as a most determined and dangerous enemy, not of our Church only, but of our State, of all our civil rights and liberties; nothing was too sanguinary, nothing was too inhuman, for her to attempt for the sake of recovering her lost authority. And it is well known what part religious discord among Protestants had in the troubles of the last century; and that the contest, which this had fomented, ended in the

Jurisdiction given be *over the Clergy of the Church of England in those parts* and none other, all reasonable pretence of suspicion seems to me to fall to the ground.

D 3   subver-

subverſion of our civil and ecclefiaſtical Conſtitution, and produced all the calamities and injuſtice, which parties inflamed with religious zeal, and irritated by mutual injuries, inflict, when they have power, on each other. After ſuch convulſions of government, where religion and politics have been ſo much blended, it is not eaſy ſoon to conſider them apart; to diſtinguiſh between religious and political principles; and to determine what degree of reſtraint is to be laid on thoſe, whoſe principles are adverſe to the State: What the ſuffering party will be very apt to think oppreſſive and vindictive, the others will repreſent as meant only for public ſecurity and peace. And while the memory of ſuch events is recent, and the animoſities ariſing from them ſubſiſting, it is but too probable, that men's paſſions will always carry them to improper lengths, and make them impoſe

pofe on their adverfaries too hard conditions.

But it has been the happinefs of our
times to be removed far enough from
thofe days of confufion, for us to be
exempt from the paffions, which in our
anceftors were very natural; and to under-
ftand much better than they did the nature
both of Civil and Religious Liberty. For
the improvements of liberty in both kinds
have gone on together, as from their
connection might reafonably have been
expected; the fubject has been difcuffed
in all its parts by the ableft hands; and
the juftice and utility of Toleration is
now as much acknowledged by all reafonable well-informed men, as any maxim
refpecting Public Religion and Civil Government. The chief caufes alfo of political
difagreement between the Diffenters and
ourfelves have long ceafed; from the

Revolution

Revolution we have been all embarked on
the same bottom of the Settlement then
made; and they have had the merit of
being, both from principle and intereſt,
conſtant Friends to it, and to the Succeſſion of the preſent Royal Family. We
have from that time conſidered their intereſts as united with our own in the cauſe
of Civil Liberty, which has for its foundation that Settlement and Succeſſion;
and it much concerns both us and them
not to be perſuaded by any unjuſt ſuſpi-
cions, or party violence, that we are not
ſtill Friends, and our great intereſts ſtill
the ſame. Our Anceſtors of the laſt century might be in ſome meaſure excuſeable,
if they were intolerant, from want of
ſufficient knowledge of the ſubject, and
from the natural workings of human paſſions. But our paſſions have not been irritated; we have had all poſſible informa-
tion; it may be expected therefore, that
we

we fhould act conformably to reafon and to juftice.

It will I prefume appear, that we have fo acted; and that the Toleration enjoyed by the Diffenters from our Eftablifhed Church has been perhaps more complete, than has been enjoyed in any other country by thofe under the fame predicament; complete I mean in Fact, though not hitherto complete by Law. For when public affairs appear to have been well fettled, and have gone on in a courfe of permanent tranquillity; there is always a reluctance (fometimes too great) in making any alteration in them. Men do not always diftinguifh, and often it is not eafy to diftinguifh, the good and beneficial parts of fuch regulations from thofe, which are unneceffary, and grown perhaps inexpedient; they know, that the whole taken together was productive of

good

good, and are therefore afraid of touching any part of it. Alterations in laws never keep pace with the change of circumstances, which are continually fluctuating; the inconvenience must be very apparent, and grow pressing, before they can be obtained; in most cases a change of opinions and manners must long beforehand gradually prepare the way for them.

In conformity to the settlement of our Civil Liberties, Toleration was granted to the Dissenters; nothing could be more reasonable and more just. It was granted on terms, which I apprehend were then satisfactory to all parties; ease of conscience was sufficiently consulted, the peace of government sufficiently secured*. Since

that

* The Dissenters dwell with pleasure on an expression of one or two great men, who have said, that

by

that time, the religious opinions of the
Diffenters themfelves have changed, they
now cannot or do not chufe to fubfcribe
to thofe opinions, which their Anceftors
held, and to which they did not object to
fubfcribe as a condition of their Toleration. What has been the confequence?
The condition has never been exacted;
and they have enjoyed the benefits of the
Toleration-Act to this day as fully, as if
it had not made part of it. For I believe hardly a fingle inftance could be
produced, when fuch inftances were di-
ligently enquired after, of a Diffenter's
having fuffered for not complying with
this condition of the Law. A fingular

by the Toleration-Act their Public Worfhip was
eftablifhed. It had certainly every degree of Legality
given to it, under the conditions prefcribed, by
whatever name that is expreffed; which is of very
little confequence. See Furneaux's Letters to
Blackftone, p. 23, 24, 2d edit.

proof

proof this of the tolerant difpofition both of our Civil and Ecclefiaftical Governors.

However, the Diffenters wifhed to be exempted from this condition by Law, from which they had been before exempted only by Connivance; and a few years ago applied twice to Parliament for this purpofe, in both which applications they were unfuccefsful. I confefs, my Lord, at the time I much wifhed, that thefe applications had been complied with. Permit me to fay, with all deference to our Legiflature, which was of a different opinion, that they feemed to afk only what was reafonable, what was confiftent with the general principles of Toleration; that it could do no harm to allow them that by Law, which they had long enjoyed in Fact, and of which in future nobody ever thought of depriving them. Perhaps the fate of thofe petitions

tions did not wholly depend on their own merits, but on some circumstances of the times, which had an unfavourable influence on them. If such an application be again made, I cannot help expressing my hopes, that it will meet with a more favourable reception : this only is wanting to render the Toleration of this country with respect to the Dissenters complete.

For although by the Corporation and Test Acts they lie under some disadvantages, I do not conceive they suffer any injury. I profess, I do not understand any general indefinite claim of all men indiscriminately to the Civil Offices of their country; or that the State may not exercise her discretion concerning the persons, to whom she may chuse to delegate any part of her authority. In fact, this is done with respect to all Offices; certain qualifications are required, which

6   exclude

exclude thofe who have them not. There certainly is a confiderable connection between a Civil Government and an Eftablifhed Church; they have a mutual influence, and the form of one ought to be, and generally is, adapted to the other. Hence we fee, that among Proteftants in Monarchical countries, the Form of the Church has been for the moft part Epifcopal; in Republics, that has been alfo Republican. Church Government will have a relation to political principles; it is unneceffary to fay, that it has had in our own country. The Conftitution of our Church is analogous, is adapted to our Civil Conftitution; the principles of the Diffenters concerning Church Government are ill adapted, are unfavourable to fome parts of it. Without recurring invidioufly to paft tranfactions, though there are among the Diffenters numbers of able and honeft men, who

3   would

would difcharge any office which fhould be committed to them moft unexception- ably, yet the general operation of thofe principles, when carried to the degree, to which even now we fee them carried, is not favourable to the whole of our pre- fent Conftitution in Church and State, which are not without reafon confidered as connected in their interefts. To ex- empt men from penalties, which they do not deferve, is one thing; to delegate to them authority is another; the firft is a matter of juftice, the latter of favour and difcretion; which the State may furely refufe to do, if fuch authority be likely to operate to her own prejudice. Of this the State muft judge, and act accord- ingly *.

* I confefs, neither the Author of *the Plan of Lectures on the Principles of Nonconformity*, or his *Ca- techumens*, if they agree with their Teacher in all his opinions, appear to me proper perfons to exercife Civil Authority under our Prefent Conftitution.

The

The Diffenters, by being incapable of Civil Offices, lie undoubtedly under a Difadvantage; a difadvantage perhaps as little felt in this country as poffible, where Induftry is branched out into fo many forms, and offers fuch a choice of ufeful and reputable employments. But it does not feem, that they can more juftly complain of an Injury, than all thofe perfons who are difqualified, for want of fufficient property, from executing different Civil Offices, in almoft all of which in proportion to their rank a certain amount of it is required; than thofe, for inftance, who are excluded on this account from the Houfe of Commons. Numbers of perfons under this incapacity would no doubt make excellent Members of Parliament; and it is not more their fault not to be worth 300l. a year, than it is the Diffenters' fault to hold religious opinions inconfiftent with thofe of the Eftablifhed Church.

If

If certain perfons are unfit to execute Civil Offices, this unfitnefs, whatever may be the caufe of it, whether poverty, opinion, or any other circumftance attending them, is a fufficient ground of their exclufion. Bad effects, produced by religious opinions, are not lefs to be prevented, than other effects equally bad arifing from other caufes.

Our Anceftors, my Lord, had the merit of granting Toleration to Proteftant Diffenters; but the public dangers from Popery were then, and continued long after, too alarming, to admit of the Papifts being comprehended in a plan of religious pacification, and of thofe Laws being repealed, the rigour of which could only be juftified by extreme neceffity. Time and a change of circumftances feem to have in fome meafure difpelled thefe dangers; we have now little to apprehend

E

hend from the attempts of that Religion
againſt the State. It is a fortunate circumſtance of our days, that in them a
conſiderable body of our Countrymen,
who were before conſidered by the Laws
as enemies to our Religion and Government, and treated as ſuch, have obtained
the confidence of the Legiſlature ſo far,
as to be relieved from ſome of the hard-
ſhips under which they laboured, and
to be in part admitted to us as Fellow-
Citizens and Friends.

For however popular it may be in this
country to hold up Popery, as an object
of abhorrence, it ſurely is not reaſonable
to ſuppoſe, that it can never be entitled
to any degree of Toleration. It may be
thought, as a matter of ſpeculation only,
that, provided the profeſſors of it no
longer breathe the ſame ſpirit of independence and hoſtility, provided by their
ſolemn

folemn declarations and conduct they give us affurance of their being good fubjects, Reliques and Images and Tranfubftantiation have little to do with the State; that men's follies and abfurdities, if they are harmlefs to others, are not proper objects of legal reftraint; and that it is having a very contracted notion of Toleration itfelf, to extend it in the ampleft form to one fet of men, and to withold it entirely from another, fuppofing that both might partake of it confiftently with public fecurity. It might be thought, that Popery might live as amicably with Proteftantifm in this country, as it does in many parts of Germany and in Holland.

But although all this may be true in Speculation, the Practical Statefman muft take in other confiderations. The reafon of the thing is not always enough

for

for him to act upon. Before such alterations are made, opinions and prejudices muſt be conſulted; which laſt are
abated only by time and experience.
We may ſee how ready people are to
take the alarm in ſuch matters by what
has paſſed in Scotland on this very ſubject; the laſt century could hardly have
produced any thing more violent. Without proceeding further, it may be prudent and neceſſary to wait and ſee the
effect of a partial relief, both on the
opinions of the people at large and the
conduct of the party relieved; for it
certainly requires ſome experience to be
perfectly aſſured, that Popery will not
make an ill uſe of any liberty which
ſhould be granted to her, conſidering
her old reſtleſs ſpirit, and the indefati-
gable zeal ſhe has always ſhewn for
making proſelytes.

The

The Penal Laws againſt Popery, which diſgrace our Statute-book, have indeed been rendered almoſt harmleſs by the humane and tolerant ſpirit of this country. The moſt ſevere and oppreſſive have been ſuffered to lie dormant and to grow ob-ſolete; they have hardly ever been called forth of late years, except now and then to ſatisfy the mean and vindictive purpoſes of private malice; and the Magiſtrate either finds ſome evaſion not to execute them at all, or does it with reluctance. Unreaſonable Laws, where the puniſh-ment is out of all proportion to the offence, for the moſt part, in free coun-tries eſpecially, defeat themſelves; the general good ſenſe and humanity of a people are revolted at them, and by pre-venting their effects almoſt repeal them.

There cannot be a ſtronger evidence of the humane and tolerating ſpirit of the

E 3   nation,

nation, than this connivance in the cafe both of the Papifts and Diffenters, which has in a great meafure fupplied the imperfection of our laws; and of this fpirit I believe the Clergy partake in as large a proportion as any clafs of men in the community. Our Predeceffors in the Church may many of them, have had their full fhare of the intolerant character of former times; but if there be a feature in the character of the prefent Clergy peculiarly diftinguifhing, it is that of good temper and moderation towards other fects of Chriftians; which difpofitions have grown more general among them, and been continually extending themfelves even to the prefent times.

Amidft the illuftrious patrons of Religious Liberty, fome of the moft eminent have arifen from the bofom of our Church; to name no more than Bifhop Taylor of

6

the laſt century, and Biſhop Hoadly of the preſent. The cauſe of Toleration in favour of thoſe, who diſſent from us and diſapprove of our Eſtabliſhment, has never been pleaded more earneſtly or more ably, than by ſome of the Miniſters of the Eſtabliſhment itſelf.

And at this time, if we are to judge from all appearances, what can be more reaſonable and moderate than the diſpoſitions of the Clergy towards our Diſſenting Brethren? Can an inſtance be produced of the Biſhops who oppoſed their late applications to Parliament, ever exerting any act of authority to diſtreſs them? Has the Eccleſiaſtical Juriſdiction in the hands of any ſubordinate Officer ever been employed for this purpoſe? Do the Clergy in their Sermons treat the Diſſenters with want of charity and candour; or endeavour to inſpire their congregations

with

with bitternefs or diflike to them? Are
their Writings from the prefs compofed
with a fpirit of bigotry and party, and
filled with fatire and invective? I profefs,
I know of no Plan of Lectures on Conformity, which can be produced as a
counter-part to that, which we have feen
on Non-conformity.

May this moderation, my Lord, always
be the diftinguifhing character of the
Clergy of the Church of England; it is
a character the moft conformable to the
fpirit of their Religion; it will do them
the greateft honour with all wife men,
with all true friends of univerfal Chriftianity. May this moderation continue
to influence every part both of their
public and private conduct. Men may
be good Chriftians in other Churches as
well as in our own; but if we are ftudious
to make Profelytes that are worth having,

this

this moderation is an argument of the moſt conciliating kind; it is even alarming to thoſe, who in this reſpect are our competitors. It is found neceſſary on this very account to put the Diſſenters on their guard againſt us; we are become dangerous to them from our mildneſs *. Nothing, my Lord, which I can add, will be paying ſo high a compliment to our Church.

* See Plan of Lectures, Preface, p. 4.

LETTER

LETTER IV.

On the Ecclefiaftical Jurifdiction.

IN Societies, my Lord, which are numerous, whether Civil or Religious, many Regulations are neceffary, many perfons in Office to fee that they are obferved; without them neither the Form or Spirit of fuch Societies can fubfift; their parts will fall into confufion, the purpofes defigned by them will not be anfwered.

It is not my intention to enter into any of the arguments, deduced from Scripture on the Form of Church-Government, which were debated with fuch violence in the laft age. To whatever opinion

different

different parties may be inclined on thefe
arguments, it feems pretty apparent, that
neither Chrift or his Apoftles meant to
prefcribe minutely thofe regulations, by
which the future Church fhould be governed in the feveral countries where it
was to fubfift. What we meet with in
Scripture are intimations and examples of
their practice concerning this Government
rather than direct commands; we do not
fee the form of it delineated at full length,
and accurately expreffed in all its parts, as
the Syftem of the Jewifh Church was by
Mofes in his Law, but only fome general
Out-lines of it: the Divine Wifdom
probably making this difference between
a Religion, which was appropriated to a
certain People, to a certain Country, to
a certain Temple, and that, which was
to be diffufed over the face of the earth,
and to take in the various nations of it,

with

with all their differences of climate and manners.

Many things in the regulation of Chriſtian Churches are certainly left at large to be provided for by Human Wiſdom; and I have therefore always conſidered the Government of Civil and Religious Societies as much on the ſame footing; and reducible, wherever the expreſs divine direction is not apparent, to the ſame principles. For God deſigned Man both for Society and Religion; they are both of them equally of his appointment. It is as much his will, that thoſe Civil Laws be obeyed, by which our Lives and Properties are ſecured; as it is, that we ſhould believe thoſe Truths and obſerve thoſe Precepts, which more immediately conſtitute our Religious Duty. But the particular means, by which theſe

3   purpoſes

purpofes are to be obtained, the particular
regulations, which will beft produce them,
are left in both cafes to be determined
by Human Wifdom, and to be accom-
modated to the different circumftances of
the Societies, for which they are wanted.
Men lie under the fame obligation to
preferve the purity and influence of Religion in making Ecclefiaftical Regulations; as they do to confult the Social
Happinefs of Mankind in making Civil
Laws.

Without recurring to divine right, nothing furely is a more natural mode of
governing the numerous Body of Clergy
belonging to a confiderable nation, than
to appoint fingle Men, with fubordinate
Officers, out of their own number to
prefide over them in different diftricts;
that is, to govern them by Bifhops. I
do not fee the impropriety of this mode

of

of governing in any country; but if it be
thought, that there should be a fort of
analogy in all countries between the Ecclefiaftical and Civil Conftitution, I fhould
fay, that in our own the Epifcopal Form
was more proper than any other for the
Government of the Church, from its
being moft analagous to that of the State.

To this Form of Church-Government
a Jurifdiction is annexed ; Courts of Judicature are held, and juftice adminiftered on certain matters, cognifable in
thefe Courts by the Laws of the Land.
We fhall beft judge of the prefent merits
or demerits of this Jurifdiction with refpect to the Nation at large, of its proper
limits and extent, by confidering the Authority from whence it is derived, and its
Operation as it is now adminiftered.

There

There is no perſon at all converſant in our Hiſtory, who does not well remember the perpetual diſputes and violent convulſions, occaſioned in the earlier periods of it by the adherence of the Clergy to their Roman Law; by their claims of exemption from all Civil Judicature; and by their daring incroachments on the power of the State. Eccleſiaſtical Juriſdiction was then indeed hoſtile and formidable; and it required all the policy and firmneſs of our ableſt Princes to withſtand and to repreſs it. The memory of this may ſtill prejudice us againſt all Eccleſiaſtical Authority; we may perhaps conſider the Old Papal Juriſdiction as the parent of the Preſent; though the deſcent has gone through ſo many generations, and through ſuch a change of fortunes, that hardly a feature of it remains the ſame.

For

For when our Church was once united with our Civil Government, the whole Authority of both from that time flowed from the fame fource; there were no longer fubfifting in the fame country two inconfiftent Powers; that of the Church became (as it ought to be) fubordinate and dependent. But for many years after our feparation from the See of Rome, neither did our Civil or Ecclefiaftical Authority wear that mild and humane afpect, which we now fee in it; the Church was indeed no longer an enemy to the State; but when the State was arbitrary, it was no wonder, if the Church fupported by it was oppreffive; they advanced gradually and hand in hand (as was to be expected) to that happy temper, by which they are at this time both diftinguifhed.

The'

The Ecclesiastical Law of this Country is now, not the Pope's, but the *King's; it makes part of the General Law of the Land, and is derived from the same Authority; the Courts, where it is administered, are subordinate, and controulable by the Civil Courts, if ever they exceed the limits prescribed to them. In this respect therefore the Ecclesiastical Jurisdiction stands clear of all exception.

The matters, which by the laws of our country are the Objects of this Jurisdiction, are some of them ecclesiastical, as the Rights and Discipline of the Church; some of a mixed nature, as Cases of Marriage; and others purely civil, as Wills and Administrations. The first are the natural and proper objects of it. Mar-

* Blackstone's Introd. Sect. 3.

F   riage,

ìiage, being with us not a mere Civil, but partly a Religious Contract, may not unnaturally fall under the fame cognifance. But there can be no reafon, from the nature of the thing, why Teftamentary Bufinefs fhould be tranfacted, or the difputes relating to it decided, in thefe Courts; and that it has been fo, has only arifen from the affumed power of the Church of Rome over the difpofition of Private Property, by which the Mode of Difpofing became then cognifable by Ecclefiaftical Authority; and from the permiffion of the General Law of the Land, that this bufinefs fhould continue to flow in the fame channel.

But however foreign part of our Ecclefiaftical Jurifdiction may be to Religion, either public or private, it is a matter in itfelf of no great importance. The principles, on which fuch bufinefs is

6   tranf-

tranfacted, and caufes decided, are equally
certain with thofe of the Common Law-
Courts, fome of which have a concur-
rent jurifdiction in thefe cafes; they are
equally confonant to the General Law of
the Land; and the perfons prefiding are
often the fame with thofe who are in-
trufted with Civil Authority. The Judge,
who prefides in a Confiftory Court as
Chancellor, or his Surrogate, often exe-
cutes, and is generally from his fituation
qualified to execute, the powers of the
Municipal Law, as a Juftice of Peace.
The decifions then of thefe Courts are
authorifed by the General Law of the
Land; and the Ecclefiaftical Magiftrates
are of the fame clafs and rank of men, to
whom that Law often delegates fome of
her own merely Civil Power. The
Clergy of England are confidered by her,
and juftly, as equally Citizens with all
the reft of her people, and as equally fit

to

to be trufted with a degree of Civil Authority proportioned to their rank in the
community; to which indeed they are
attached by every tie, that can make men
interefted in its welfare.

If thofe matters, which are certainly
not the natural and proper objects of Ecclefiaftical Jurifdiction were removed
from it to that of our Common Law-
Courts, I confefs I fhould have feen no
material objection to it, (except the tranf-
ferring of certain Fees from one fet of
Officers to another fhould be thought
fuch) had not a much better * judge
than myfelf been of a different opinion.
" It muft be acknowledged (fays he) to
" the honour of the Spiritual Courts,
" that though they continue to this day
" to decide many queftions, which are

* Blackftone, B. iii. Ch. 7. Vol. iii. P. 98.

" properly

" properly of temporal cognifance; yet
" juftice is in general fo ably and impar-
" tially adminiftered in thofe tribunals,
" (efpecially of the fuperior kind) and the
" boundaries of their power are now fo
" well known and eftablifhed, that no
" material inconvenience at prefent arifes
" from this jurifdiction ftill continuing
" in the antient channel. And, fhould
" an alteration be attempted, great con-
" fufion would probably arife, in over-
" turning long-eftablifhed forms, and
" new-modelling a courfe of proceed-
" ings that has now prevailed for feven
" centuries."

The Forms indeed of thefe Courts are
on the Roman plan, and confequently
different from thofe of the Common
Law; but there are other Courts befide
the Ecclefiaftical, which proceed accord-

F 3   ing

Ing to the fame forms, efpecially the
Court of Chancery. We need not hefi-
tate in giving a preference to the mode of
Legal Proceeding delivered down to us by
our own Anceftors ; but if any inconveniences be fuppofed to arife from the
other mode, thefe are not peculiar to the
Ecclefiaftical Courts, but operate alfo
elfewhere in cafes much more important.

Excommunication, my Lord, is unfortunately the inftrument, by which the
Ecclefiaftical Jurifdiction is to affert its
authority. I have no fcruple in faying,
that the inftrument is improper and bad.
As fuch I believe every Ecclefiaftical
Judge ufes it moft fparingly, and never
employs it without neceffity; but as no
Jurifdiction can fubfift, where an obfti-
nate Party may fet it at defiance with
impunity,

impunity, the neceffity will fometimes occur, when it muft be employed; if fubmiffion can be obtained by no other methods, it muft be obtained by that, which the Court is impowered to ufe in the laft refort. Befide the fpiritual part of Excommunication, a part which never fhould have been applied to thefe purpofes, many civil difabilities, and thofe of the moft ferious kind, are immediately incurred by it; * and ' at the end of forty days, ' if the offender does not fubmit to the ' fentence of the Court, the Bifhop may ' certify fuch contempt to the King in ' Chancery, from whence the Writ *de* ' *excommunicato capiendo* is iffued to the ' Sheriff of the County; who fhall there- ' upon take up the Offender, and imprifon ' him in the County Goal, till he is re- ' conciled to the Church, and fuch recon-

* Blackftone B. 3. Ch. 7. Vol. iii. p. 102.

F 4 ' ciliation

' ciliation certified to the Bifhop.' I have
often wifhed, my Lord, that the Law in
this refpeét was altered; that the effeét,
or part of the effeét of Excommunication
might be obtained, as it might eafily be,
without the previous and unbecoming
formality of fpiritual cenfures. Suppofing
an Ecclefiaftical Judge were empowered in
cafes of contempt, where he muft now
excommunicate, after forty days to require
by a proper inftrument the imprifonment
of the party in contempt, from the Sheriff
or a Juftice of Peace, on the fame conditions of delivery, when his fubmiffion is
certified; a part only of the confequences
of Excommunication would be incurred,
but a part fufficient to fecure obedience
to the Court; the remedy would be had
more eafily, and lefs reluétantly employed;
the offenfive ufe of fpiritual cenfures
would be avoided; and the Ecclefiaftical
Jurifdiétion would owe its fupport, juft-

as

as much as it does now, to the intervention of the Civil Power *.

Ecclefiaftical Rights and Difcipline
feem the natural and proper objects of
Ecclefiaftical Jurifdiction. The Laity
are concerned indeed in many of the firft;
but the decifions in thefe cafes are the
decifions of the Law of the Land, and
fome of the temporal Courts have a con-
current Jurifdiction, fo that parties may
make their choice; to thefe indeed almoft
all matters of confequence are at this time
carried of courfe. The Laity have little

---

* Since I wrote this, I find, that a propofal of
the fame kind was agreed on in Convocation 1714,
and intended to be offered to Parliament, that it
might pafs into a law. Wilkins's Conc. Vol. iv.
p. 654. This defign dropped on Queen Anne's death,
which happened foon after. Such a propofal had
before been mentioned in Convocation 1580. ibid.
p. 300.

now

now to apprehend from Church-Autho-
rity, except the prefentment of a Country
Church Warden for any irregularities of
life be efteemed formidable. Canons
framed by a Convocation have been de-
clared by the greateft * Lawyer of his age
not binding on the Laity; and juftly de-
clared fo, becaufe not iffuing from the
Legiflature, to which they are fubject;
and the Ecclefiaftical Courts, if they
feem ever fo little to exceed their due
bounds, are immediately corrected by the
Courts of Common Law.

I am perfuaded, that no reafonable man
among the Clergy would wifh to carry
Church-Power over the Laity a ftep
beyond where it is at prefent fixed;
but in what relates to the internal regula-

* Lord Hardwicke—fee Burn's Preface to Eccl.
Law.

tion

tion and difcipline of the Clergy themfelves, and the due performance of Ecclefiaftical Duties, the cafe is very different.
Let the Power of the Church over others
be little, or none at all ; but let her have
enough to controul and govern her own
immediate fubjects; to make *them* do
their duty, and to correct *their* delin-
quencies. In doing this, let her not be
checked at every ftep by the interpofition
of the Common Law Courts, which in
thefe cafes feem to ufe rather more than
* " a parental authority;" let not every
flight occafion be embraced of transferring
the matter in queftion to another judicature. It furely is not confulting the
intereft of the Public at large to weaken
the hands of the Officers of the Clergy
with refpect to their own body ; to throw
embarraffments and difficulties in their

* See Black. B. iii. Ch. 7. Vol. iii. p. 103.

way,

way, when they would prevent or correct
abufes, of which the Laity are naturally
enough very ready to complain, but of
which perhaps the weaknefs of Church-
Authority in the hands of its Governors
is the caufe.

The Refidence of the Clergy, for inftance, is undoubtedly good as a general
principle; but is fubject from the nature
of it to a variety of exceptions, which
can never be all provided for by any
written Law, and which fhould be left
to the difcretion of fome fuperior. The
Bifhop is certainly the perfon, who is the
proper judge of them; and we may I
think prefume, that few men in that ftation would be fo unreafonable as to infift
on it indifcriminately, without any confideration of circumftances, in all cafes.
As the matter now ftands, a Bifhop would
find it for the moft part a very difficult,

3   if

if not an impracticable, attempt to compel by courfe of Law a Clergyman to refide on his Benefice. To expect, that the fubordination of the Clergy fhould be as ftrict as that of the Army, would be putting perhaps too ftrong a cafe. But what fhould we fay of an Army, where the Commanding Officer had not power to make a Subaltern join his regiment * ?

The Bounds of the Ecclefiaftical Jurif-diction have indeed been contracted on all occafions; hardly any opportunity of doing it has been omitted. That it is

---

* Next to the Clergy themfelves, it might be thought, that there could not well be a more proper fubject for Ecclefiaftical Jurifdiction than a Parifh-Clerk; but the doctrine of Weftminfter-Hall feems to be, that he is a Temporal Officer, and confequently not amenable to it. Burn's Eccl. Law. Title Parifh-Clerk. Pitt and Evans. Parker and Clerke. Peak and Bourne.

ftripped

ftripped of its old ufurpations is happy for
us all; that it is no longer what it once
was, formidable to the State and independent of it; incompatible with the
national welfare, and oppreffive to individuals. It is happy for us, that it is not
now, what it was for many reigns even
of our Proteftant Princes after the Reformation, a partaker with them of power
too ill-defined, too roughly exercifed to
be confiftent with public Liberty. But
we may poffibly have fallen into the
oppofite extreme; and by lowering it too
much may have rendered it weak and in-
effective with refpect to that, which is its
proper province. It muft be confeffed,
that it came from a fufpicious parentage;
it is no wonder, that after fo many generations fome may ftill look on it with a
jealous eye, and hardly yet think themfelves fafe from it; though at this time
we might almoft as well, from the fame
refemblance

refemblance of features, be afraid of the Court of Chancery.

While the Ecclefiaftical Judicature decides well and agreeably to our General Law on thofe civil matters, which are ftill committed to it, it is a thing of great indifference from what fpecies of Court thefe decifions iffue. With refpect to any Cenforial Power over the Laity, what remains to this Jurifdiction is trifling, I had almoft faid contemptible; and it would perhaps be as well, if even that remnant were taken away. But when we were getting rid of the fuperfluous and offenfive parts of Ecclefiaftical Authority, we feem to have gone too far, to have cut away without diftinction, and not to have been fatisfied with reducing its growth, till we left it without vigour fufficient for the internal government of our Church.

LETTER

LETTER V.

On the Provision of the Clergy.

IN every country, my Lord, the Provision for any Class of men in it must depend on the rank that Class holds in the community, on the abilities required from it, and on the industry, riches, knowledge, and manners of the country itself. Where industry is branched out into a variety of employments, which furnish numbers with a comfortable and reputable subsistence; and where from the riches of the nation Merit in every branch of it meets with suitable encouragement; there every Profession must offer to those who engage in it adequate rewards, such as are proportioned to those

of

of other profeſſions which are nearly of
the ſame rank. Otherwiſe, amidſt ſo
general a competition, that which is below
the market-price will find no cuſtomers,
and be deſerted.

The proficiency of a nation in know‑
ledge and the arts of life, makes the
demand for knowledge in almoſt all pro‑
feſſions proportionably greater, multiplies
the requiſite qualifications, and increaſes
the labour and expence of acquiring them.
The manners alſo of a people very much
affect all profeſſions in it; and regard muſt
be had in them to many things, which at
firſt ſight may appear of little or no con‑
ſequence: it is very certain, that in almoſt
all of them appearances muſt be to a
certain degree conſulted, faſhion complied
with, and a decorum preſerved, founded
more on opinion than on the nature of

G   things

things themselves. These confiderations acquire ftrength, the higher the rank is which any particular profeffion holds in the community, and the greater the abilities which are required from it.

There never was perhaps a Country, where fo wide and inviting a field was laid open for Induftry of all kinds as our own; where there was fuch a choice of ways of life, all of which, if properly purfued, afford a reafonable profpect of convenience and comfort. And as this is a country, where riches (and great part of them of the moft valuable kind, riches acquired by induftry) abound and are diffufed throughout the people, Merit of every kind bears here a higher price than elfewhere, and every owner has reafon to expect he fhould be better paid for his abilities.

We

We need not I believe fear incurring the imputation of partiality, by suppofing this nation as far advanced in all kinds of ufeful knowledge, poffeffed in as high a degree of all thofe improvements, which enlarge the human mind, and produce convenience and elegance of life, as any which ever yet exifted. The eighteenth Century will probably always be con-fidered as a period, when knowledge and arts abounded and flourifhed; and where-ever the improvements of that period are recorded, our own Country will I am per-fuaded hold there a diftinguifhed place: But in fuch a country the individuals of different profeffions muft keep pace with the ftate of general improvement; igno-rance in any of them becomes more difgraceful; the public, to whom pro-feffions are accountable, will lefs bear with it.

The

The advancement indeed of our knowledge, the variety and perfection of our arts, the extent of our commerce, and the multiplicity of our connections render Government in every part of it, whether foreign or domeſtic, complicated and difficult. Government is moſt immediately affected by theſe cauſes; but they operate alſo in ſome degree on all the higher profeſſions of our country.

All the foregoing circumſtances concur in forming our national Manners. Induſtry, Riches, Arts, and Knowledge, wherever they flouriſh, as they do here, civiliſe men; give them ſocial virtues, and qualities, which make life convenient and agreeable. But as all human advantages are attended with their reſpective evils, they civiliſe men to exceſs, and make them pay too much regard (for ſome regard is due) to the diſtinctions in Society,

Society, which they naturally create.
Family and Wealth command amongſt us
a degree of reſpect; the owners of them
are entitled to it, ſo long as they do not
diſgrace their pre-eminence by unworthy
conduct. From thus naturally connect-
ing reſpect with theſe advantages of fortune, we almoſt appropriate it to theſe
only; we connect them ſo much together,
that we cannot conſider them enough
apart to beſtow reſpect, where we ſee a
total want of worldly advantages. In any
ſtation to which reſpect is due, the pureſt
virtue and the beſt abilities will not
command it from the vulgar, if it be
accompanied by what they have been
taught to think mean; if it want that
external decency of appearance, which
they expect from it.

I ſhall now, my Lord, apply the ob-
ſervations I have been making to the

Proviſion

Provision assigned by the Law to our Clergy, and offer such considerations as shall occur concerning it, and which appear to me to have some weight in determining on its general propriety; whether it be sufficient for the purposes designed, or too little or too much; whether it be well distributed; whether the nature of the property be convenient; and on the whole, whether it be consistent with sound Policy and public Welfare. But I must premise, that my reasonings will only apply to those readers, who think it of importance to the public and private happiness of mankind, to their present and their future existence, that the Belief and Influence of the Christian Religion should be preserved; and who consequently think it necessary, that an Order of men should be set apart to teach and to administer it, without which its Belief and Influence cannot be preserved;

5

to thofe, who will allow, that the Public Profeffion of Chriftianity fhould be fupported by Civil Government, and a fuitable Provifion for its Minifters affigned by it.

It is not lefs neceffary, that this Provifion fhould be adapted to the circumftances of our Country and Manners, than that of any other clafs of men in the community. Their Qualifications muft bear a proportion to the general ftate of Knowledge and Improvement; their expence in acquiring thefe qualifications will alfo be increafed in proportion to the Riches of the country and the expence of living in it; they will be invited by the advantages of other profeffions, before they engage in that of the Church; when they have engaged in it, their way of living and external appearance muft be regulated by prefent manners, and the provifion for their families by the prefent meafures of education and fubfiftence.

G 4 The

The higher ranks in this country confift for the moft part of perfons of improved underftanding; a general degree of knowledge is diffufed alfo throughout the whole mafs of the people; the Preacher, who is to addrefs them, fhould certainly be himfelf competently furnifhed with it, in order to acquit himfelf with fatisfaction to them, or with any degree of reputation to himfelf. Mere Knowledge, a fund of proper topics for religious inftruction, is not only requifite, but good Judgement alfo in felecting, and applying them, together with fomething conciliating in the manner of their being conveyed. Men of good fenfe are difgufted and difappointed at hearing Religion fupported by futile, infufficient, and injudicious arguments, which are apt to have an unfavourable effect on their general belief of it. And to all hearers fuch inftruction comes recommended by being agreeably conveyed, by

5   having

having a reasonable degree of attention paid to the manner, in which it is both composed and delivered.

If it be thought, that all this is not wanted to satisfy the Country-Congregation of a small village; there are cases, where it is wanted in a much higher degree. In this land of liberty Religion is attacked with as little reserve as it is defended; the wit and the acuteness of Infidelity are employed against it without mercy. That this should be the case, I do not think just matter of complaint; but it is fit, that the defence should be managed as ably as the attack; that the Body of the Clergy, the natural defenders of Religion, should always afford men qualified for this service, and at least equal to their adversaries. It is their business, and a business which requires the best abilities and most extensive knowledge,

ledge, to refcue the truths both of Natural and Revealed Religion from the fophiftry, mifreprefentation, and ridicule, with which they are often treated; and to eftablifh them on the firm foundations of reafon and good fenfe. There is a connection between all parts of knowledge; they give mutual affiftance to each other; for a Clergyman to be poffeffed of that, which is merely profeffional, is not enough to make him an able defender of Religion.

It is well known, that the Education preparatory to the Clerical Profeffion is attended with a very confiderable expence from the earlier parts of life; an expence nearly the fame with that, which is neceffary for the other Liberal Profeffions; and which has for fome years increafed together with the increafing riches of our country.

The

The Emoluments then of the Clergy should bear a due proportion to those of other professions, that require nearly the same abilities, are attended with the same expence, and hold the same rank in the community. As it is, amidst the numbers of which this Order consists, there are always in it many men of the first abilities; the greater part from decent and reputable, many from the most considerable families in this country. Should there be a great and evident disparity to the disadvantage of this profession compared with those others, can it be expected, that men, who might form reasonable prospects of success in any other profession from their abilities or connections, will engage in this? The profession must itself be lowered; it must be deserted by those, who are best qualified by their abilities for the first stations of it; and by those, whose personal rank and

connections

connections would tend to give it confideration and refpect.

The better parts, for inftance, of the Law and the Church are made out of the fame materials, are compofed of men of nearly the fame rank, fortune, and education. Is it improper, that a Clergyman of merit in his profeffion fhould acquire in it what he might probably have himfelf acquired at the Bar; and what others in moft refpects his equals do acquire there? Have they not the fame claim to fuccefs in their different ways? Should fuccefs be thought reputable in one cafe, and invidious in the other? Is it lefs proper, that he, who fet out a private Clergyman, fhould become a Bifhop, and have a feat in the Houfe of Peers; than that he, who fet out a private Barrifter, fhould be an Attorney or Sollicitor General, a Judge, or a Lord Chancellor?

‘ But

' But such success in the Law is a more
' certain proof of great professional merit,
' than in the Church.' It is admitted.
I do not mean to complain of want of
rewards in the Church, or of the great-
ness of them in the Law. I know no
character, which deserves more from this
country, than that of an able, learned,
and upright Legal Magistrate; all honours, all wealth are well bestowed on
him; but they far exceed, as perhaps
they ought to do, those of the Clerical
Profession.

There has been no source both of No-
bility and Riches more fruitful, or indeed
more truely honourable, than that of the
first offices in the Law; the Church also
has her Honours and her Wealth. These
Honours make part of our Civil Constitution; they are not transmissible to families;
why, under this restriction, they are improper,

proper, as the Rewards of a Profeſſion, I confeſs I cannot diſcover. As to Eccleſiaſtical Wealth, where ſhall we find the families, that are built on it? Where ſhall we trace up Modern Riches to an Eccleſiaſtical, as we continually do to a Legal Anceſtor? The Wealth of the Church can in theſe days be very rarely accumulated to any amount; and if it be thus accumulated, it is not abſorbed by her, but flows back again into the ſociety at large.

Take away the rewards of this profeſſion, and men of good proſpects will betake themſelves to other paths of life; they will be determined by the ſame motives in the deſtination of their Children. It is a ſubject, in which prudential conſiderations muſt have their due weight; thoſe profeſſions, which are moſt reputable and promiſing, will of courſe be moſt purſued;

fued; no one profeſſion has a right to claim a preference with reſpect to the virtue of its members, when in all of them, by acting well, men may be equally good, may alike do their duty to God and to their Country.

But dropping the conſideration of what may be called the prizes of the Clerical Profeſſion, it ought to afford to all its members a Subſiſtence adapted to the rank they hold, to the office they diſcharge in the community. They muſt if poſſible maintain an appearance, which will procure them ſome reſpect from the bulk of the people, who are governed by appearance; whatever looks like meanneſs, whatever expoſes them to contempt wilI not only lower the perſonal regard paid to them, but will hurt their miniſterial character, will in ſome meaſure diſqualify them from acting with effect in it.

For

For in our prefent ftate of manners it is in vain to expect, that the people fhould ever treat Poverty, however refpectable in itfelf, with refpect; it depreciates in their eyes every other quality.

The Profeffion therefore fhould afford all its members a reafonable profpect of fuch a fubfiftence, as will fupport the rank they hold, and the appearance in the world that is expected from them; and this muft be eftimated from our prefent habits, from our prefent modes of thinking; what would provide decently for a Clergyman in Switzerland, or in the remoteft parts of our own Ifland, is not a meafure applicable to the greater part of the Englifh Clergy.

Their income is from the nature of it more known than that of other profeffions; it is expected, that they fhould live

in

in a way proportioned to it; and even thofe, whofe income is more affluent, have it on this account lefs in their power to make confiderable favings, than men in moft other fituations of life.

Upon the whole; a probable judgement may I think be formed, whether the general Provifion for the Clergy be more than fufficient for their reafonable demands, from the following confiderations. Are they in general able to improve the fortunes of their families? To leave their Children in a better fituation, than they were in at the fame age themfelves? To qualify them for employments of a fuperior rank and of higher pretenfions, than their own? It feems to me clearly, that they are not able; and therefore, if their character be not extravagance, for which as a general charge I know no reafon, their Provifion is not more than fufficient;

it

it only leaves their families, where it found them.

That there should be a difference of rank and income among the Clergy seems as proper, as in almost all other ways of life, where the same difference generally obtains. To rise from lower degrees in a profession to higher, either from merit or long standing in it, is the natural progress of human life. It is necessary for the purposes of government and subordination; it is proper, as a spur to emulation, an encouragement to merit, and a reward of long services. The inequality however may be greater than these purposes require, and it may not always operate in such a manner as to encourage merit, and to reward long services.

It is certain, that interest and connections will have their weight in the distri-

6   bution

bution of Church-preferments. Succefs in the Law is, as I before obferved, a more certain proof of profeffional merit. It may fometimes happen in the Church, that great advantages may be obtained, where there is little or no merit; it may alfo happen, that the moft deferving may be left in obfcurity and neglect. The more common cafe is, that great Eccle-fiaftical Advancement is the joint effect of both intereft and merit; yet there are numberlefs inftances, where the latter alone and unaffifted procures what is comfort-able and affluent; fome, where it attains the higheft dignities of the Church.

It is fit, that the revenue of its Go-vernors fhould be ample; equal to the rank affigned them in our country; nei-ther is there any reafon, as I faid before, why the reft of the Clergy fhould all be on a level: but the difproportion feems in

many

many inftances too great. All fhould
have what is fufficient for a decent Sub-
fiftence; without it men are cramped,
difcouraged, and in fome meafure difqualified for the duties of their office. None
fhould have from the Church (for of
men's private fortunes I am not fpeaking)
fuch an excefs, as leads rather to luxury
and diffipation than the regular and ferious difcharge of their clerical functions,
and makes the comparative fituation of
others humiliating and unpleafant. In
many inftances accidental caufes have contributed to a difproportion between the
income of preferments and the duties
attending them. A change of circumftances has often taken place, fince that
diftribution of Church-revenues was
made, which ftill fubfifts. Villages,
which were inconfiderable, are become
populous; Towns have arifen on fpots,
which were not inhabited; and thofe

places

places are not uncommonly the worſt provided for by legal rights, where the Parochial duties are the moſt laborious.

But this inequality of the conditions of the Clergy will not be thought ſo great, as at firſt ſight it may appear, if we attend to one conſideration. Competence is a relative thing; and is meaſured by that, which the education, habits, and connections of each individual have taught him to expect, and have made in ſome degree neceſſary to him. The numerous body of our Clergy is compoſed of a great variety of materials; if the bulk of it be produced from the middle ranks of life, thoſe nearly on a footing with itſelf, yet the moſt conſiderable families in this country contribute likewiſe their part, and there is a large portion, whoſe origin is far below it. The younger Son of a Nobleman or Gentleman of property

is

is not *for him* perhaps better provided for by what is thought great Preferment, than the Son of a Mechanic, whofe Father was juft able to get him into the Profeffion, is by a fcanty and obfcure Country Living: the natural wants and expectations of both, at their fetting out in life, may perhaps be equally anfwered; both may have what is to them competence in the fame degree. And thofe, whofe origin is low, whofe connections are mean, are the perfons, that will of courfe moft fuffer in the unequal diftribution of ecclefiaftical revenues; the others will be the gainers by it.

The greateft part of the Provifion of the Clergy arifes from Tithes; a fort of property appropriated to them in this country from high antiquity; and adapted in many refpects to an Owner, whofe profeffion it is not to cultivate land, and who

is

is only Tenant for Life. It is managed with eafe, without the trouble or expence of a continued courfe of agriculture. It is not liable to the injury, which land will fuffer from a carelefs or diftreffed predeceffor. It is as much a diftinct property, as the land from whence it arifes; it was neither purchafed by the Landlord, nor is it rented of him by the Tenant. Yet this property has alfo its inconveniences. The interference of it with that of the Occupier of the land is unpleafant, and productive of difputes, to be avoided if poffible in all cafes, but efpecially in that of a Clergyman and his Parifhioners. Difputes between them leffen or deftroy his influence, and in fome meafure defeat the purpofes of his paftoral character. Tithes have been thought not favourable to induftry and improvement, in the trouble and expence of which men will not fo readily

H 4 engage,

engage, when another is to fhare in the
advantages. There muft be fome truth
in this, though it does not feem from the
ftate of this country, as if it had produced
in any confiderable degree this effect.

Where Inclofures are made by Act of
Parliament, (a mode of Improvement, by
which the national ftock of wealth arifing
from the produce of land is greatly increafed) in the new diftribution of property,
this inconvenience is ufually avoided by
giving a feparate portion of land as an
equivalent for Tithes. The Clergyman's
property, thrown into this feparate form,
no longer interferes with that of his Parifhioners, and it is liable to no objections
as unfavourable to induftry; but the general
expediency of it may admit of fome doubt,
as in this form it may become lefs convenient to the owner, and lefs adapted to
the fituation of a Tenant for life.

The

The property of Ecclesiastical Bodies consists for the most part of lands granted for Lives or a Term of years. The small Rents Reserved on those estates is an income of the most certain kind, least subject to variation or accident; and therefore peculiarly fitted to answer the stated demands of such Bodies. Fines on the Renewals of these Grants are of a more contingent kind; and must be considered as such by those, to whom they belong. This part of the income of the Church has been in general managed with great moderation; on these renewals much less than the real value, often not more than half of it, has usually been demanded. It is I think much to be wished, that this moderation should always be preserved; the holders of this kind of property have an equitable claim to it, from its value having been long estimated and the price determined on this presumption. Men

are

are alfo governed in fuch things more by habit, than by ftrict notions of right; and pay a larger fum, which they expect to pay, with lefs reluctance, than a fmall one which is due by the cleareft right, but to the payment of which they have been not accuftomed.

Somewhat of the fame objection may be made to eftates for Lives or Years, which I before mentioned as applicable to Tithes, that they may be in fome degree unfavourable to improvement, the advantage of which is not clearly received by the improver, but muft in a fmall part be continually repurchafed at fucceffive renewals. And there have been very lately a few inftances of a partition of this kind of property by the intervention of the Legiflature fomewhat fimilar to that, which has been made in Tithes. An average of all the profits of a Leffor has been com-

puted

puted for a fufficient length of time, and
this made an annual charge, as a Fee-farm
Rent, on the Eftate, which is enfranchifed
and becomes Freehold to the Leffee; a
proper part of this new Rent being re-
ferved in Corn, to guard againft the fluc-
tuation of the value of money. The
objection on the fcore of Improvement is
taken away; difputes on the terms of
Renewal prevented, and the revenue to
the Ecclefiaftical Owner is rendered certain inftead of contingent. Thefe advantages are obvious; but the objection to
this mode feems to be, that the Agreement between the Leffor and the Leffee
being made once for all on the footing
of the prefent value, the former and his
fucceffors will be excluded from all advantages of future improvement.

All fuch changes of property both with
refpect to Tithes and Ecclefiaftical Leafes,
muft

muſt be made on proper terms, adapted
to each particular caſe; for no general
proportion can be laid down, which will
be applicable either to the one or to the
other. To induce an alteration of theſe
kinds of Property on any other plan would
occaſion great confuſion and injuſtice;
conſidering the length of time they have
ſubſiſted in their preſent form, and how
widely they are diffuſed over the nation.
For they are not confined to Eccleſiaſtical
Owners; the Impropriations poſſeſſed by
Laymen, the Grants made by Civil Cor-
porations and private Proprietors, fall
under the ſame deſcription, and are liable
to the ſame objections.

The Engliſh Clergy do indeed ſucceed
the Roman Catholic Clergy of this country
in part of their poſſeſſions, but it is only
in part of them; a large portion was at
the Reformation and afterwards diverted
to

to other purposes, and does not belong to our Present Clergy, who have very different merits with the public. The share of their Predecessors before that time was large out of all proportion; and this will appear in a much stronger light, if we consider, that the whole of the property of the Church bore then a much greater proportion to the national wealth, than the same property would do at present; and must have operated accordingly. At this time, when the Wealth arising from Industry, Arts, and Commerce is so prodigiously increased since the period of which we are speaking, the same quantity of Landed Wealth will no longer have the same influence and effect.

It was perhaps the Master-piece of Roman policy to secure the dependence of her Clergy, by declaring them free from all civil ties, by rendering them incapable

capable of forming natural connections, and thereby detaching them from the countries, to which they belonged. Men, who difclaimed the authority of Civil Judicatures, who had no domeſtic pledges to bind them to their country, we juſtly treated with fufpicion and diffidence. On this account the Roman Clergy were not properly Citizens; on the contrary, as the fituation of the Engliſh Clergy is directly oppoſite in thefe refpects to that of their predeceſſors, they perhaps have as juſt pretenſions to the character of Good Citizens, as any of their Fellow-Subjects; they are led to be fo by every natural and civil intereſt. They profeſs by the principles of their Church an entire dependence on Civil Authority; to that they owe the Proviſion on which they ſubfiſt, and the Rank which they hold in the community; and perhaps there is no claſs of men in our country, whofe domeſtic

and

and family connections attach them more to the public welfare of it.

To such a Clergy, my Lord, it is, I should apprehend, confiftent with every principle of found Policy to affign a Provifion in all refpects fuitable to their office and rank; if the Chriftian Religion be of importance to mankind, if the Public Profeffion of it be fit to be fupported, and a certain Order of men neceffary for the adminiftration of it: thefe things I have taken for granted in this inquiry. There is perhaps room for many improvements in the nature and diftribution of this Provifion; but there feems little reafon to think, that it is on the whole too large, that the profpects of this Profeffion are too inviting, or that it is fet above the level of thofe others, which are filled by perfons of the fame original fortune, education, and rank. A Barrifter, a Phyfician, Gentlemen

Gentlemen of the Army or Navy, a Merchant, with tolerable qualifications and prudent conduct, have all of them a reasonable prospect in this country of obtaining for themselves a decent Subsistence, a competent Provision for their families; any degree of eminence usually gives them Reputation and Affluence; and high Honours with great Wealth are the prizes, which often fall to the share of the most fortunate and most distinguished. With respect to the Clergy, Family-Honours and excessive Wealth are out of the question; but I confess I can see no reason, why an English Clergyman has less pretensions to all other advantages of a liberal profession, than those, who set out with him from the same beginnings in life, but as they advance take other paths in it.

.LETTER

LETTER VI.

On the Learning of the Clergy, and the Freedom of Inquiry.

GENERAL Learning, my Lord, is in fome degree profeffional to the Clergy; their education ufually affords the means of it; and their way of life, removed for the moft part from the more active and bufy employments of the world, gives them opportunities, which other men have not, of cultivating and extending it. The Learning immediately required of them is certainly that, which has a direct reference to their duties, without which they cannot difcharge them ably and effectually. But, as I before obferved, almoft all kinds of

I   knowledge

knowledge have fome connection, and are ·
ufeful mutually to each other; and if
there are parts of it, the utility of which
is lefs apparent, we may at leaft admit its
claim even in thefe to fome regard as a
liberal accomplifhment.

We muft judge from the Writings of
our Clergy, on religious fubjects, compofed either for the Public in general or
for the Inftruction of their particular
congregations, of their merit in that
Learning, which immediately belongs to
them.

And if there be a fort of Merit, to which
the Clergy of England have a more indifputable claim than to any other from
the times of the Reformation downwards,
it is certainly that of Clerical Learning.
I think I may venture to affert, that the
Clergy of no country have produced from
that period to the prefent fo many able

Writers

Writers on the fubject both of Natural
and Revealed Religion; that the truths
and duties of both have been no where
confirmed, explained, and taught with
more knowledge, with founder reafoning,
with more good fenfe; that the attacks
made on both have no where been repelled
more ably; and the caufe of Proteftant
Chriftianity againft the Church of Rome
more fuccefsfully defended.

I do not apprehend, that the prefent
Clergy would on inquiry be found in
thefe refpects unworthy of their Predeceffors. The ftate of Learning, like that
of other human things, is fubject to continual change, is affected by the circumftances of times; our modes of thinking,
and of expreffing our thoughts differ in
different ages; the demand alfo for particular forts of Learning is different, according to the queftions, which are agitated,

　　　　　, and

and the opinions, which prevail. View-
ing things in this light, I am not fenfible,
that our prefent Clergy are unworthy
Succeffors of thofe eminent and venerable
Men in that particular, where their reputation ftood higheft; that this merit of
our Church is not tranfmitted down entire
to our own times.

For much of controverfial Learning
there is no longer the fame demand. At
the Reformation and long after it, we
were contending for the very effence of
Religion; our moft valuable rights, as
Chriftians and as Citizens, were concerned
in the difpute; it was neceffary to direct
our principal force to this quarter. Proteftantifm was alfo unfortunately divided
in itfelf; and much unneceffary controverfy about trifles between the different
fects of it engaged men's attention and
abilities, which would have been better
employed

employed againſt that Church, from whoſe tyranny they had all been juſt reſcued; or in eſtabliſhing and defending the great truths of our common Chriſtianity. Happily for our times theſe controverſial weapons have been little wanted: Popery in this country is no longer an enemy worth contending with; and the Diſſenters we have, I think, long conſidered as Friends, between whom and ourſelves no cauſe of animoſity ſubſiſted, though ſome difference of opinion. Our Modern Clergy have, I believe, much leſs controverſial learning than their Predeceſſors, becauſe there has been much leſs occaſion for it: a happy circumſtance for us; Religious Controverſy, as it has been uſually carried on, being more apt to irritate the paſſions of the reſpective parties, than to convince their judgement.

The

The Writings of our Predeceffors were more voluminous than ours; the controverfial manner naturally led to this; it was alfo the fafhion of the times; Readers as well as Writers had, if you pleafe, more induftry, certainly more patience, than at prefent. Almoft every kind of compofition affumed a prolix form, which fuited the public tafte, and with which it was therefore the inclination and intereft of the writer to comply.

It muft be confeffed, that in thefe days we have had an opportunity of profiting by the labours of our Predeceffors, and we may be reafonably expected to have improved upon them. In works of mere genius Predeceffors afford little help; in thofe of mere fcience they afford the greateft. The fubjects of Religious Learning are of a middle nature, in which great

6   advantage

advantage is to be derived from those, who have gone before us; though not so great as in subjects strictly scientifical. And I presume, that we shall not appear to have made an ill use of that stock of Religious Knowledge, which we have thus inherited.

The great truths both of Natural and Revealed Religion, and the duties result-ing from them were perhaps never more ably discussed than by the Divines of our Present Church; these subjects are for the most part well understood, and the reasoning employed to establish them is just and convincing. For different ages have different modes of reasoning; it should seem as if the Human Mind were constituted differently at one time and another, from the different manner, in which it is at such times affected, We in many instances reject as futile and

I 4

fallacious

fallacious that reasoning, which our anceftors were ready to take for ftrict de-
monftration. Things, which they confidered as important enough to occafion
the moft ferious and unhappy difputes,
we now treat, and many of them very
juftly, as the mereft trifles. We are
perhaps hardly fair judges of our own
comparative merits; but furely there is
in the reafonings of the prefent age a
degree of good fenfe, which we do not
find fo generally in our earlier Writers,
and ftill lefs in thofe of other countries.
If there be any truth in this, it is in no
inftance more true than on religious fubjects; they are treated by our ableft
Writers, and of fuch I am fpeaking,
with more good fenfe and found reafoning,
than they have ever been before.

If we confult the theological writings
of other Chriftian countries, we fhall, I

3   believe,

believe, foon be convinced of this with refpeȼt to them. But even in reading fome of the moſt celebrated Authors of Antiquity on philofophical fubjeȼts, which are of the fame nature and often coincide with religious fubjeȼts, I have frequently been led to refleȼt on the apparent inferiority of thofe Authors, with refpeȼt to juſt reafoning, to the more eminent of our modern Divînes. We muſt diveſt ourfelves of fome prejudices, before we can venture to prefer an Engliſh Sermon, even of the firſt rate, on a philofophical or moral fubjeȼt to a Dialogue of Plato, an Eſſay of Cicero or Plutarch; but with all reverence to thofe great men be it faid, there will probably appear in the former, not perhaps the fame elegance of form and language, but more good fenfe and juſt reafoning. It is not, that the abilitíes of any Modern Divine are fuperior to thofe of thefe illuſtrious

Ancients;

Ancients; but our Religion has given us a more perfect knowledge of these subjects, and this is an age, with us at least, of better reasoning.

Good sense and a just manner of thinking arrange and employ the materials of what is commonly called Learning; make Knowledge useful and applicable to the important purposes of life. With the learning and knowledge also, which immediately belong to their Profession, our Clergy are eminently furnished. An acquaintance with general History, as connected with Revealed Religion, as well as with the particular History of the Religion itself, with Christian Antiquity, with the opinions and practices of Christians in different ages, especially those relating to our own country, is all of it in some measure necessary to Clerical Learning; but the great source, from whence all our

Knowledge

Knowledge of Revealed Religion is derived, are the Holy Scriptures. In thofe other auxiliary branches of learning there is, I believe, no reafon to complain of any deficiency; but in this moft effential one, the ftudy of the Holy Scriptures, the languages in which they were written were perhaps never better underftood. With refpect to the Old Teftament, a new field of Criticifm is laid open in it, to which our Anceftors had no accefs, and which will much contribute to reftore that part of our Scriptures to their integrity, and to render our knowledge of them more accurate. For Commentaries on the whole Body of the Scriptures, we are indebted to many learned men of our own and of other countries, who have gone before us; their opinions thus collected are valuable and deferve to have weight with us; but we do not fail to judge for ourfelves and to improve on

their

their labours; particular parts have been selected, and illuftrated by able and mafterly Criticifm, and we are continually adding to our ftock of Scriptural Knowledge. We fhall foon be furnifhed with moft of the proper requifites for an undertaking, which would do honour to the prefent age, as well to thofe who fhould authorife it, as to thofe who fhould conduct it with fuccefs; a New Tranflation of the Scriptures. You, my Lord, have pointed out the way to us; and it will be well, if we can follow You at fome diftance.

Although the fpirit of Controverfy between different denominations of Chriftians be in our days much fubfided, yet there never was more frequent occafion to repell the attacks made on Chriftianity itfelf. Such is the Freedom of thefe times and of this country, that no fubject is treated with lefs referve and tendernefs, than

than the Religion of it; it is attacked in all ways, by fubtle and acute reafoning, by learning, by the lighter forts of writing which are agreeable and captivating; all readers are addreffed in a way fuited to their refpective taftes; ferioufnefs, ridicule, and irony are employed, as beft anfwers the purpofe; which laft is more offenfive, becaufe it is unneceffary. It is fufficiently plain, that with refpect to Chriftianity at large the Freedom of Inquiry is not cramped by any influence of the Church or any coercions of the State. It is, I believe, the general fenfe of the Clergy, that when the truth of Religion is called in queftion and attacked, civil reftraints are foreign to the defence of it; that reafon and argument are the only arms to be ufed for that purpofe; and that on thefe its defence may be fafely refted, if it be, what they truft it is, founded in truth and derived from God. To
them,

them, who are entrusted with the public administration of it, the province of defending it naturally belongs; and from them have issued, as occasions have required, the ablest Apologies for Christianity, which the world ever saw: its general principles have been established, objections in all their different forms have been answered, with more solid learning, sounder reasoning, and more good sense, than perhaps in any country, since the first propagation of it.

The learning and abilities of the English Clergy, not only in defence of Christianity against its adversaries, but in their general treatment of Religious Subjects, in their knowledge and interpretation of Scripture, in their explanation of the doctrines and duties of the Gospel, have always been held in high estimation by most of the other Protestant Countries

in

in Europe. In Germany, as I am well-informed, Englifh Divinity ftands high in reputation; and is confidered as a neceffary part in the courfe of Clerical Studies to thofe, who profefs to attain in them any great degree of proficiency and eminence.

Far be it from me, my Lord, to detract from the merit of our Diffenting Brethren for their joint labours with us in the common caufe of Chriftianity. On the contrary, I have always confidered them as Friends and Affociates engaged in the fame work; I have always feen with pleafure our agreement on the great truths and duties of Religion; and think it for the moft part a recommendation, both of their performances and ours, where the differences fubfifting between us are not marked; when the party, from which they come, cannot be diftinguifhed.

In

In such performances the merit of our Diffenters will always be acknowledged by every impartial judge of Learning, by every friend of Chriftianity; in fuch we fhall both of us do real fervice to mankind, and acquire lafting reputation; while Pofterity will defpife and forget moft of the paltry Controverfies, with which our differences are continued and fomented.

The Reftraint laid upon Opinions, the want of Freedom of Inquiry in religious fubjects, is an inconvenience conftantly charged on Eftablifhments; in this refpect it might be fuppofed, that thofe, who diffent from our Church, would have greatly the advantage of us. Yet in fact even the Diffenters can hardly propofe their opinions with more freedom, than the Clergy of the Eftablifhed Church; they can hardly cenfure that Church more

unrefervedly,

unrefervedly, than fome of her own Members take the liberty of doing. A Clergyman does not indeed always in fuch cafes profefs himfelf the Author to the public by name; but it is generally as well known and underftood, as if the name were written in capitals.

It muft be confeffed, Opinions are fometimes propofed, not very confiftent with the former folemn Profeffions of their Authors. But who now ever hears of any thing like coercion or punifhment? Is Herefy now a crime, that occurs in our Ecclefiaftical Courts? Is it in any danger from Convocations, which are become of all public Affemblies the moft unimportant and moft innocent? In truth, the imputation of inconfiftency is perhaps in the prefent ftate of things the moft powerful reftraint of opinions, that contradict thofe, which have the fanction of public authority.

K

,thority. The liberty, thus taken and carried to fuch a degree, as we fometimes fee it, may not itfelf be very confiftent with the fpirit of our Old Church and with the Forms of her Legal Conftitution; but in this as in other matters men are relaxed in their ways of thinking; the general opinion favours this liberty; which in fact is enjoyed as fully, as if it were exprefsly allowed by the Laws of our Church; certainly as fully, as any moderate and reafonable men can defire. It is like our Toleration, which, though not complete by Law, yet has been completely exercifed in Fact.

Every fort of Liberty may be carried to an extreme; but without a confiderable degree of it, in religious as well as other fubjects, learning is fettered, prejudices are continued, and improvement is ftopped; it is better, that it fhould fometimes exceed

exceed its bounds, than be too much reftrained; the field is always open for reafon and good fenfe, to check what is extravagant and abfurd. Of this moderate liberty the Clergy of England have made an excellent ufe in the promotion and improvement of every branch of religious knowledge. Neither have they any reafon to fear, that thofe reftrictive Laws, which have lain fo long dormant and obfolete, fhould ever regain their life and vigour; on the contrary, the progrefs of things will certainly be made the other way, and Written Laws will at length accommodate themfelves to Prevailing Opinions. It is laudable and ingenuous in our own Clergy, when occafions offer, to point out defects and to fuggeft amendments in our Eftablifhment; it is honourable with refpect to the Church herfelf, which allows this liberty to her members. But fuch writings fhould preferve that de-

corum

corum and moderation, which is confiftent with the relation the Authors of
them bear to the Church, of which they
treat. Satire and Invective againft her
will do no credit either to the good fenfe
or good temper of a Writer of any denomination; but muft come with peculiar
impropriety from thofe, who have pro-
feffed allegiance to her laws, and who
fubfift by her appointments.

The religious Learning then of the
Englifh Clergy feems in no danger of
having its progrefs ftopped by unreafonable reftraints; its growth has been accordingly vigorous, and its produce
abundant. But Learning, ftrictly fpeaking
profeffional, is not only what may be expected from fuch a Body of men; we
may reafonably hope to find among them
a general literary character, a degree of
proficiency, and in fome inftances ₁ of
eminence,

eminence, in almoſt every branch of knowledge. Their own education, and the province which often falls to them of educating others, open a field in which they may purſue different parts of learning; though that, which properly belongs to them, be their chief object. And this is connected with knowledge of almoſt every kind; a relation ſubſiſts between the various branches of it; they mutually aſſiſt and promote each other; and by their general connection the mind of a ſpeculative and ſtudious man is im-perceptibly led from one purſuit to ano-ther. In all the different views, which may be taken of Religion, in order to eſtabliſh it and to obviate the objections which may be made to it, it is hard to name a part of knowledge, that may not have its uſe; and for compoſition of every kind on religious ſubjects, it is obvious, how re-quiſite it is for the Clergy to be well

K 3   acquainted

acquainted with the beft Authors of all ages; as patterns of good writing and juft reafoning, if they hope to acquit themfelves with reputation and effect. On the whole it is not unreafonable to expect, that there fhould be a general ftock of ufeful and liberal knowledge lodged, as a depofit, in the hands of the Clergy.

In fpeaking of numerous bodies of men and the qualifications required from them, we fpeak of them always in the bulk. Every individual will not anfwer the general character; great eminence is, and ever was, confined to a few; if the greater part of a profeffion be competently qualified, and the number of thofe deficient comparatively fmall, it is perhaps all, that can in the nature of things be expected. The different fituations alfo of the Clergy, and the different ranks of people with whom they are to officiate,

make

make their general qualifications requisite in very different degrees: in some situations they are all wanted; in others the best and most excellent would be thrown away; they would be inapplicable and useless.

From the times of the Reformation downwards, the reputation of the Church of England has certainly stood high for Religious Knowledge and Useful Literature. Have the Holy Scriptures in any country been more studied, or better illustrated by sound learning and true criticism? Have the truths and duties of Christianity been any where explained more ably, or more faithfully inculcated? Has Christianity itself been any where more successfully defended by the united force of reason and of learning? Has religious knowledge been any where prosecuted with less restraint? How far the Body of

K 4   our

our Clergy may now be qualified to keep up the reputation of their Church may perhaps in some measure be collected from the foregoing letter; at least it may not become me too peremptorily to decide on it; but, my Lord, I hazard nothing in saying, that we have certainly some names now among us, which will do no discredit to the most illustrious of our Predecessors.

LETTER

LETTER VII.

*On the Public Forms, and on the Duties
and Manners of the Clergy.*

WHOEVER, my Lord, has well
considered the difficulty of com-
posing Addresses to God, fit for public
use, not unworthy of the Being who is
worshipped, and yet intelligible to the
meanest of his worshippers; whoever
has well considered the judgement and
sobriety of mind, which are necessary on
a subject, in which we are so apt to in-
dulge a warmth of imagination and to
mistake it for piety; will not hesitate in
determining, whether it be most expedient
to have the addresses, made to God in
Public Worship, conceived in certain

3   general

general and prescribed Forms, or to have them left to the discretion and abilities of each particular Minister. To perform them, when thus left to the Minister, with tolerable success does indeed require a degree both of abilities and discretion, which can by no means be expected from the greater part of those who officiate; and it is obvious, how often reasonable men must in that case be disgusted with what is injudicious and improper.

* ' It is said to be unreasonable, that ' Christian Ministers should be confined ' to a stated Form in their Prayers more ' than in their Sermons;' as if there were not a striking difference. The Prayers pronounced by the Minister, and addressed to God, ought to be such, as all

* See Protestant Dissenter's Catechism, Part ii. Quest. 42.

the

the Congregation can join in and make their own; whereas Sermons are addreſſed to the Congregation, who are not to make them their own, but to hear and to judge of them. For thoſe, who are always inſiſting on their Right of Private Judgement, will I preſume exerciſe it upon the Sermons of their Miniſter, and not take all that he teaches them implicitly and upon truſt. The abſurdity, if there be any, in a Sermon is only the Miniſter's; in Prayers, the Congregation muſt adopt it, or muſt not pray. Not to mention, that the ſubjects of Moral and Religious Inſtruction admit of prodigious variety; whereas thoſe of Prayer are comparatively few in number, and therefore eaſily reducible to ſtated Forms.

It can hardly ever happen, that in any thing, which has been a matter of diſpute, one ſide can be exempt from all inconveniencies,

veniencies, and its oppofite attended with no advantages. But not to trouble You, my Lord, with taking the unneceffary pains of proving, that in Public Worfhip the advantages attending ftated Forms vaftly preponderate, I will beg leave to offer fome reflections on the Forms of our own Church.

They are certainly on the whole good: I do not mean good with refpect to the particular religious opinions they exprefs, for that is a confideration of quite another kind, but with refpect to their Manner and Language ; they are inftruments well adapted to promote true and rational piety. God is addreffed in them with fimplicity, yet with dignity; a juft fenfe of his tranfcendent attributes, and of our dependence on him, pervades the whole of them; they comprife all the various modes of addreffing him, for the fupply

of

of our wants, for pardon of our fins, for benefits received, which our relation to him as Men and as Chriftians renders proper and neceffary; the diftribution and expreffion of thefe different modes is well calculated to awaken and to keep up our attention; there is warmth enough in them for the rational worfhipper, though not perhaps for the enthufiaft; and the ceremonies, with which our forms are accompanied, are few, decent, and in-telligible. The Language alfo, in which they are compofed, is for the moft part peculiarly proper for the purpofe; the Liturgy and Englifh Bible have given, as a fort of ftandard, a degree of permanency to our whole language; they have in fome meafure fixed our tafte with refpect to that, which is proper for the public offices of Religion; and the caft of anti-quity, with which they are tinctured,

only

only ferves to make them more fimple and venerable.

But allowing our Public Forms all this merit, for one party to fuppofe them perfect, and for the other to reprobate them for not being fo, is equally unreafonable. Perfect they could not be; and if that had been poffible, they could not have appeared fo to different men of different opinions. They would be unlike all other human performances, if they were not capable of improvement in a long courfe of time, from fubfequent knowledge, from continued experience, from repeated obfervation, and let me add, from the cenfures of thofe who diffent from us. A Revifion of our Forms by Authority would, my Lord, as I conceive, do honour to our Church; it would give it the true merit of being really

more

more perfect, at the expence only of parting with an imaginary notion of perfection.

An impropriety has in fome inftances arifen from a change in the manner and time of performing the public fervices of the Church. Some of thofe, which were originally intended for different times, are now ufed together; for this reafon they appear not well united; there are unneceffary repetitions now in them, which were not fo in their feparate ftate; and the whole is rendered too long and lefs uniform.

The Scripture, though we allow it all to be of divine authority, yet is not in all its parts equally fit for public and popular ufe. The Compilers of our Liturgy appear to have been of this mind; and have accordingly wholly omitted

feveral

ſeveral parts of it in the courſe of Leſſons. It would be perhaps better, if ſtill more were omitted, and replaced by other parts more uſeful and edifying. Some of the Apocrypha in particular, to which indeed we attribute no divine authority, has ſo much the air of legend and fable, that it by no means deſerves a place in the ſervice of our Church.

Thoſe parts alſo of Scripture, which occur moſt frequently in our public worſhip, and are ſelected for the time, when our churches are fulleſt, ſhould be the moſt edifying, ſhould be the leaſt liable to be miſconſtrued, and miſapplied by the ignorant, either in their faith or practice. In this view, I cannot help thinking, that even ſome of the Pſalms are not proper for a part of the ſervice, which occurs ſo frequently. I ſhould ſuppoſe too, that Leſſons might be ſelected

for

for Sundays and Holidays more improving than the prefent, more applicable to the belief and conduct of a Chriftian.

If ever fuch a Revifion fhould take place, many alterations, few perhaps confiderable, throughout the whole of our Liturgy would offer themfelves, which would undoubtedly render it more perfect; more approved by the judicious Members of our own Church, and lefs exceptionable to thofe, who are difpofed to cenfure it.

The Public Inftruction of the Church of England is fuch as muft always do her honour. It is on the whole able and edifying; the truths and doctrines of Chriftianity are explained with knowledge and good fenfe; the duties of it are inculcated with earneftnefs. Controverfial fubjects, ufelefs and indeed unintelligible to moft

L   congre-

congregations, are wifely almoft banifhed
from our pulpits ; the difcourfes delivered
from which tend to make the hearers
good Chriftians in general, rather than
zealous members of a particular Church,
and partizans of a particular fect of
Chriftianity.

I have not, I believe, faid too much of
our Public Inftruction in general; but
the beft part of it is certainly excellent
in its kind : the firft-rate Sermons of the
Englifh Clergy, are probably the ableft
performances of the fort, that ever were
compofed or delivered. And notwithftanding the general complaint, perhaps
too well founded, of the infidelity of the
age, of our want of all attention to religious fubjects, there appears to be a conftant demand for fuch difcourfes, as are
excellent in their kind, and come from
Authors of known and eftablifhed reputation.

tation. In this commendation of the Sermons of the eftablifhed Clergy I would join the Diffenters with them, as I have before done on the fubject of Clerical Learning, with which indeed the compofition of Sermons is connected. They have contributed their part to the excellent collection of Englifh Sermons, of which the public is poffeffed. Theirs and ours are for the moft part fo much the fame, that they may be ufed indifferently by both of us; a circumftance which I think both fhould obferve with pleafure; for I do not wifh to magnify the differences between us: we agree in fo many things which are good and important, that I would never by choice dwell on many of the trifling particulars in which we differ.

The Sermons of our Clergy are ufually precompofed and delivered from writing; this mode and the other of fpeaking an

unwritten

unwritten discourse have, as it generally
happens in other cases, their respective
advantages and disadvantages. The first
method will produce discourses more
correct in all particulars, in reasoning,
language, and method; the latter will have,
when tolerably performed, more life and
feeling. But when congregations, especially those of the better sort, have been
long used to the accuracy and order of
discourses written and prepared in private,
they will not easily be satisfied with listen-
ing to those of an extempore Preacher;
who, except he be a man of very eminent
and superior abilities, must necessarily
produce what is far short of that, which
is the fruit of meditation and study. For
the subjects of Religious Instruction cannot
be treated before an audience with the
same ease with those, which are usually
discussed in other public Assemblies.
They are many of them of a more nice

6

and

and difficult nature; and however in-
terefting in a philofophical and religious
light the truths and duties of Chriftianity
may be thought, yet in common life
they will not engage men in the fame
degree with the popular bufinefs of the
prefent moment, ufually difcuffed in fuch
affemblies. The intereft men take in
bufinefs of this kind fupports both the
fpirit of the Speaker, and the attention
of the Hearers, and in treating it we are
by cuftom taught to expect lefs form and
accuracy.

That the Clergy fhould difcharge their
duties with knowledge and ability, as
well as be regular and punctual in them,
is of the greateft importance; but thefe
duties, however difcharged, will by no
means have their full effect, except they
be accompanied by their own Example;
except their Life and Manners be fuch,

as

as to recommend the Precepts they deliver, to evince their fincerity in the belief of thofe Truths which they profefs to eftablifh.

It is certain, they have peculiar motives for virtuous and exemplary conduct. The ftudies, the bufinefs of their profeffion naturally direct their mind to ferious objects ; it can hardly be fuppofed that the man, who is continually employed in telling others their duty, in offering to God their addreffes, which confift of petitions for the relief of our wants, and for the forgivenefs of our fins, of promifes of obedience, of expreffions of gratitude for his bleffings, fhould do all this fo mechanically and by rote, as not to make the application to himfelf, and to let it operate on his own conduct. He muft reflect, if he reflects at all, that although obedience to the commandments

of

of God be a univerſal obligation on all
mankind, yet it comes with peculiar force
on him, whoſe office it is to prevail on
others by every motive to obey him;
that the Teacher, who contradiɛts by his
own life the inſtruɛtion he delivers, and
thus defeats the effeɛt of it, muſt be in-
excuſable. And if a man cannot be
influenced by better motives, without at
leaſt a decency of charaɛter there can be
no tolerable proſpeɛt of ſuccefs in the
Clerical Profeſſion; for however corrupt
the world about us may be, and indulgent
to vice, yet a vicious Clergyman is a
charaɛter ſo very unbecoming in the fight
of all people, that it ſeldom meets with
indulgence, and certainly does not deſerve
it. So that without giving the Clergy
credit for better natural diſpoſitions than
their neighbours, it may reaſonably be
expeɛted, that their conduɛt ſhould be
better, even upon principle; at leaſt, with

reſpeɛt

respect to the world, more decent and circumspect.

But notwithstanding all these particular motives, as they are made of the same materials with men of other professions, it cannot be supposed, that in every case these motives will have their due influence. To expect, that ten thousand men will always act well, because they are Clergymen, is to expect, what the condition of human nature will not admit. That their conduct should be in general good, that their lives should be innocent, that the decorum of their character should be preserved, is a reasonable expectation. It may be expected, that the want of this decorum should not be common; and that there should be very few instances of gross and public misbehaviour. When such instances happen, and happen rarely, to infer any thing from them to the discredit

credit of the profeſſion itſelf, is not conſidering the nature of Man, the infirmities and faults to which he is liable, whatever may be the external ſituation in which he is placed.

If this be a reaſonable meaſure for eſtimating the conduct of a Body of Clergy; I ſhould flatter myſelf, that thoſe of our own Church would at leaſt come up to it; that the conduct of the bulk of them would be thought becoming their profeſſion, and the inſtances of the contrary in any groſs degree appear comparatively very rare. For in theſe caſes the numbers, of which a Body of men conſiſts, muſt always be taken into the account; and when a particular inſtance is conſidered, the proportion which it bears to the whole muſt be conſidered alſo. In this reſpect ſmaller ſects have the advantage of the predominant religion of a country;

country; their Ministers are few in number, and the very circumstance of their dissenting from the majority keeps them on their good behaviour.

Decorum in the Clerical Profession, and indeed in most others, does not depend on what is merely moral or immoral in the conduct of men, but has reference to present Manners. Prevailing habits and modes of thinking render things, in themselves indifferent, proper or improper, and give them a relative importance. Every prudent man must to a certain degree comply with these, if he would fill any station of life with credit to himself, or usefulness to others. The character of a Clergyman from the nature of it ought certainly to be marked with somewhat more seriousness, somewhat more regard to appearance even in innocent things, (for of immoralities I am not speaking)

speaking) than that of the generality of the world. But this decorum muſt be the decorum of the preſent age and of preſent manners; what our anceſtors thought ſo would with us be ſtiffneſs and auſterity, and would ſit as awkwardly on us as their dreſs.

I am ſenſible, this is not the extreme, into which our Clergy are in danger of falling, the general propenſity of the times running ſo ſtrongly another way: diſſipation and levity of character are the things in theſe days to be avoided. Yet without incurring the imputation of theſe, the manners of the Clergy may ſurely be ſuch, it is I think deſireable, that they ſhould be ſuch, as to fit them for the ſociety of the world, not to exclude them from the better part of it; an eaſe of character, added to their higher qualifications of virtue and good ſenſe,

sense, is most likely to recommend the
Religion, of which they are Ministers *.

As it is to be wished, that the instruction and example of the Clergy should
influence all ranks of men, the highest
as well as the lowest; it is surely expedient, that they should not be viewed in
a disagreeable or contemptible light by the
former; and this will not disqualify them

---

* I cannot help mentioning, what I heard from
a very intelligent Hessian Officer, of good character,
who was in England with the troops of that country
in the last war. He had been introduced to a Clergyman of eminence, one of the most chearful, polite,
and amiable men in the world ; he expressed the ut-
most surprise to me at finding him so agreeable a man;
' for, added he, as to the Clergy of our country,
' they are quite a different sort of people ; we do not
' like them at all.' The manners of the German
Clergy rendered them in general, I presume, unac-
ceptable to men of the world, and unfit for their
society.

from

from being regarded properly by the latter, who are perhaps the firſt to deſpiſe thoſe of a better ſtation, whom they ſee approach too nearly to themſelves.

An Engliſh Clergyman of Knowledge in his profeſſion, punctual in the Duties of it, and unblemiſhed in his Character, if to theſe qualifications he joins thoſe accompliſhments of general Learning, and that agreeableneſs of Manners, of which many of our Clergy are poſſeſſed, bids perhaps as fair, my Lord, to command proper reſpect, and to acquire uſeful influence with all ranks of people, as any Chriſtian Miniſter in any country, where Chriſtianity is profeſſed.

LETTER

LETTER VIII.

Conclusion.

I HAVE thus, my Lord, ventured to offer You my thoughts, as they occurred to me, with much freedom, on the Prefent State of our Church-Eftablifhment. It muft be left to your Lordfhip's judgement, and to that of the Public, if thefe Letters fhould deferve the attention of the Public, to determine, how far the reprefentation I have given of the different parts of the fubject be juft; I can only fay, that I have reprefented them in the light, in which they appear to me.

It is a fubject, my Lord, which if purfued more at large would afford room for

3   much

much difcuffion, for many different opinions; in which continual panegyric is
not to be expected, much lefs continual
cenfure to be apprehended; for if we
fhould fufpect with reafon the fincerity
of the one, we fhould reprobate with ftill
more reafon the injuftice and malevolence
of the other.   I muft repeat what I have
faid already more than once, that in efti-
mating the merit of Human Inftitutions,
and of Numerous Bodies of Men, we
fhould not raife our expectations above
the ftandard of Humanity.   The charac-
ters of all Societies, formed for the civil
or religious purpofes of mankind, will
be mixed, like thofe of the Individuals
of which they are compofed; to expect
Perfection in them implies an ignorance
of our nature; we muft take thofe for
good, which are good on the whole; and
be fatisfied, if we mean to be fatisfied in
this world, with perfons and things,
                                    where

where the defects are comparatively few, and the good confiderably predominant.

It is in this view, my Lord, and with fuch expectations only, that I have pur-fued thefe reflections. How far the Church-Eftablishment, as it now fubfifts in this country, is an Inftitution fit for the purpofes it was meant to anfwer, both with refpect to Religion and Society; how far the Clergy of England are worthy Minifters of the Religion of Chrift, and ufeful Members of our Civil Community, were the objects of my inquiry. Whe-ther I have eftimated the merits both of the Eftablishment and its Clergy by their proper meafure, whether the conclufions I have drawn are reafonable or not, others will determine; I do not pretend to pre--fcribe to them the judgement they fhall form; but if what I have faid fhall in any degree approve itfelf to your Lordfhip

in

in particular, and to any other candid,
liberal, and intelligent readers, in whofe
way thefe letters may fall; if it fhall
fuggeft to them any topics, which may
affift them in forming their own judgement, the purpofe of this addrefs will be
fully anfwered.

I am not more defirous, that fuch
readers fhould be fatisfied with thofe parts
of our Church-Eftablifhment, which appear to me good and unexceptionable, than
I am, that their attention fhould be di-
rected to thofe parts, which are capable
of improvement, and which call for it.
Though it muft be expected, that all
Human Inftitutions will have their defects; this is no reafon, why endeavours
fhould not be ufed to leffen and correct
them; to render their proportion to what
is good as fmall as poffible. Length of

M   time

time and change of circumſtances produce
of themſelves unforeſeen inconveniences
in things, which were planned at firſt
with the greateſt wiſdom; they make
what was originally well adapted to
the purpoſes intended, unfit and inapplicable; they produce improvements in
knowledge, which in juſtice to ourſelves
we ſhould adopt; ſo that Human Inſtitu-
tions of every kind will grow, from theſe
cauſes only, leſs perfect and leſs uſeful,
except they are from time to time refitted
and readjuſted.

This muſt be the caſe of every National
Church, which has long ſubſiſted; and
it ſeems reaſonable to uſe the ſame conduct with reſpect to that, as all wiſe
nations do in other parts of legiſlation;
to make ſuch alterations and amendments
in Eccleſiaſtical regulations, as any improvements

provements in religious knowledge, or change of circumſtances may require. That this ſhould be done not wantonly or unneceſſarily, will readily be admitted; but we ſurely ſeem too tender, too much afraid of moving a ſtone of our Church, as if on being touched, though ever ſo gently, the whole fabric would fall to pieces: I truſt there is in it more ſtrength and ſolidity. There might be reaſon for this exceſſive caution, if the Church were now, as it once was, an inſtrument of party, and the very name of it ſufficient to ſet half the nation in a flame; but now, my Lord, bad conſequences are very little to be apprehended on account of any wiſe and uſeful alterations, which ſhould be recommended to the Legiſlature by the Governors of our Church; they would be well received by the moderation and good ſenſe of the better part of the nation, to the inattention and indif-

ference

ference of moſt others they would be un-
intereſting. Such improvements may be
made, without affecting the great principles, on which our Eſtabliſhment is
founded, or changing its eſſential parts;
by being ſo improved its virtues would
be more acknowledged, its utility more
apparent.

. The Clergy, who act under it, have
every motive to render themſelves, what
by their character and ſituation they are
qualified to be, worthy Miniſters of the
Religion of Chriſt, and uſeful Members
of our Civil Community. Their Predeceſſors, a generation or two backward,
could not perhaps as a Body of men be
eſteemed favourable to that ſyſtem of
Liberty, which took place at the Revolution; they could not immediately
diveſt themſelves of old prejudices concerning Government. But theſe ſubſiſt

no

no longer; Civil Liberty perhaps owes more to one Great * Man of the Clerical Profeſſion, than to any other ſingle Writer of any denomination. The principles, on which it is founded, are dif-fuſed at large throughout the Clergy, and as generally adopted by them, as by any other Claſs of men. If they ſhould be charged by the over-zealous Friends of Liberty with not carrying their notions of it far enough, further than they are authoriſed by the legal principles of our Government, to that charge I believe they would plead guilty in its utmoſt extent; for they are bound by every tie of duty and intereſt to preſerve and ſupport, as far as lies in them, our Preſent Civil Conſtitution.

I reflect on this and on our Eccleſiaſti-cal Eſtabliſhment with nearly the ſame

* Hoadly.

ſentiments

sentiments. Notwithstanding the many defects and corruptions in the former, which candid men will allow, and the uncandid will exaggerate; yet when I see, that in this country we are more free, more secure in our persons and property, than the inhabitants of any country have been, whose history is transmitted to us; that justice is administered in our Courts of Law with a purity, of which there is no example; that this Constitution has in fact produced for near a century, more public and private happiness, than any government which has ever yet subsisted; I must conclude, that it is on the whole excellent, however improveable in some of its parts; that it deserves the warmest affection and most faithful support of all its members. So likewise, however injuriously our Whole Church-Establishment may be sometimes treated by passionate men; though reasonable and moderate men may think, that in some of its Parts it wants

correction

correction and is capable of amendment;
yet, when I confider its Spirit of Toleration towards other fects of Chriftians,
the Freedom with which Religious Inquiry is purfued under it, the Learning
and Abilities of its Clergy, their Literary
Productions in the Support of Chriftianity
and for Inftruction in it, with the general
Decorum and Propriety of their Manners,
I cannot help concluding, that the Prefent
Church of England on the whole deferves
the efteem and veneration of our own age,
and that it will hereafter be confidered
by Pofterity as a worthy and illuftrious
branch of Chrift's Univerfal Church.

www.ingramcontent.com/pod-product-compliance
Lightning Source LLC
Chambersburg PA
CBHW031117020726

47495CB00007B/2231